House of Secrets

A play

Peter McKelvey

Samuel French - London
New York - Hollywood - Toronto

© 1994 by Peter McKelvey

Rights of Performance by Amateurs are controlled by Samuel French Ltd, 52 Fitzroy Street, London W1P 6JR, and they, or their authorized agents, issue licences to amateurs on payment of a fee. **It is an infringement of the Copyright to give any performance or public reading of the play before the fee has been paid and the licence issued.**

The Royalty Fee indicated below is subject to contract and subject to variation at the sole discretion of Samuel French Ltd.

> Basic fee for each and every
> performance by amateurs   Code L
> in the British Isles

The Professional Rights in this play are controlled by Samuel French Ltd

ESSEX COUNTY LIBRARY

The publication of this play does not imply that it is necessarily available for performance by amateurs or professionals, either in the British Isles or Overseas. Amateurs and professionals considering a production are strongly advised in their own interests to apply to the appropriate agents for consent before starting rehearsals or booking a theatre or hall.

ISBN 0 573 01788 3

Please see page iv for further copyright information

CHARACTERS

Trevor Billingham, late twenties
Julie Pringle, about twenty
Hector Parsloe, late fifties
Sarah Higgs, late twenties
Richard Higgs, early thirties
WPS Beverley Hammond, early thirties

ACT I

SCENE 1 An autumn morning
SCENE 2 The same day, early evening
SCENE 3 A few hours later

ACT II

SCENE 1 Saturday morning, the following week
SCENE 2 The same day, early afternoon

The action takes place in a lodging house in London

Time—1990

COPYRIGHT INFORMATION

(See also page ii)

This play is fully protected under the Copyright Laws of the British Commonwealth of Nations, the United States of America and all countries of the Berne and Universal Copyright Conventions.

All rights, including Stage, Motion Picture, Radio, Television, Public Reading, and Translation into Foreign Languages, are strictly reserved.

No part of this publication may lawfully be reproduced in ANY form or by any means—photocopying, typescript, recording (including video-recording), manuscript, electronic, mechanical, or otherwise—or be transmitted or stored in a retrieval system, without prior permission.

Licences for amateur performances are issued subject to the understanding that it shall be made clear in all advertising matter that the audience will witness an amateur performance; that the names of the authors of the plays shall be included on all announcements and on all programmes; and that the integrity of the authors' work will be preserved.

The Royalty Fee is subject to contract and subject to variation at the sole discretion of Samuel French Ltd.

In Theatres or Halls seating Four Hundred or more the fee will be subject to negotiation.

In Territories Overseas the fee quoted in this Acting Edition may not apply. A fee will be quoted on application to our local authorized agent, or if there is no such agent, on application to Samuel French Ltd, London.

VIDEO-RECORDING OF AMATEUR PRODUCTIONS

Please note that the copyright laws governing video-recording are extremely complex and that it should not be assumed that any play may be video-recorded *for whatever purpose* without first obtaining the permission of the appropriate agents. The fact that a play is published by Samuel French Ltd does not indicate that video rights are available or that Samuel French Ltd controls such rights.

ACT I

Scene 1

The lounge and kitchen in Richard and Sarah Higgs' lodging house in London. An autumn morning

A DR door leads to the lodgers' kitchen. Next to this is a wall mirror in front of which stands a bureau. A window is CR and between this and the back door is a light switch. A lamp stands between the back door and the window UC, in front of which is a window seat. A telephone and drinks trolley stand UL. An archway opens on to the kitchen UL. Below this a door leads to the hall and front door

A kitchen table with chairs stands CL. Two armchairs and a coffee table are placed just to the R of DC. A photograph of Sarah's father stands on the bureau

The lounge is a touch makeshift yet resonant of old prosperity, with pictures and plates on the wall, and a modest heirloom or two in evidence

As the CURTAIN *rises, Julie is silhouetted against the back window. She laughs*

The Lights come up on Julie, young, pert and provocatively attractive, who stands talking on the telephone. She turns to sit on the window seat. Trevor sits in the armchair C reading a newspaper. He is in his late twenties and wears the obligatory ragamuffin clothes of the disaffected. During Julie's speech, Hector, of pinched, municipal stamp enters DL. He collects the waste bin from the kitchen and exits UR. When he opens the back door he lets in the muted yet distinct sound of pop music from the neighbours' hi-fi. This is shut out when he closes the door

Julie Yeah. . . . No. . . . Well. . . . I. . . . Yeah. . . . Yeah. . . . Fantastic . . . Yeah. . . . Well, you know what I mean. . . . That's right . . . Yeah. . . . What was I going to say? . . . You're joking? . . . You must joking! . . . I s'pose that goes without saying. . . .

Yeah. . . . I know . . . Listen . . . Listen, I must go. . . . No, I must. This is the landlord's phone. I'm not s'posed to. . . . 'Bye. (*She hangs up*)

Trevor You'll kop it.

Julie Mind your own.

Hector enters UR *with the waste bin which he has just emptied outside. Music continues for as long as the door is open. He crosses to the kitchen to deposit the bin and returns to the kitchen table*

Trevor (*laying aside the newspaper*) Still cleaning up, Hector?

Hector I don't mind. This is home to me.

Trevor You're a lodger.

Hector I've been here four years come next month.

Trevor You're still a lodger.

Hector I've been here nearly as long as Sarah and, and Richard have been married.

Trevor You're still a lodger.

Hector You two haven't been here more than five minutes. I'm more like one of the family.

Trevor smiles

Yes . . . I was their first lodger.

Trevor There you are. You're a lodger.

Hector (*mumbling*) I keep busy, which is more than I can say for some . . . You look smart, Julie.

Julie (*moves* DR *of chair*) I'm going for an interview.

Hector What's wrong with the job you've got?

Julie I'm only a temp. (*She sits on a chair* R)

Hector You've been one for nearly a year now. You're a contradiction in terms, that's what you are. Yes.

Julie I quite enjoy being a temp. You never know what will happen. But in the main you're typing all day. Just sitting there; typing all day. Some days are all right. It's not a taxing job. You don't have to think.

Hector Don't you?

Julie No. Well, not really. (*She takes up the newspaper*)

Sarah enters and sits on the window seat. She is in her late twenties and middle class. Even her casual clothes have a touch of style

Hector You know that er . . . what's his name? Rudolph Valentino.

He was considered to be the greatest screen lover who ever lived.

Trevor groans

When he died he was only thirty-one. Thousands of women mourned all over the world. Yes. Two thousand women claimed that he was the father of their child.

Trevor groans

Two thousand! Yet do you know that doubts have been cast on his manhood? His second wife claimed that the marriage was never consummated.
Julie Fancy that.
Sarah You telling stories again, Hector? You'll be late, you know.

Richard enters DL from the front door and stands L of the table. He is aged thirty, dressed smartly in a business suit and carrying a briefcase. He is clearly irritated

What's wrong?
Richard The car's broken down. Of all days . . .
Sarah Try not to get het up, dear. Phone the garage.
Richard They won't repair it straight away, will they? They'll want to tow it in, jack up the bill.
Sarah You'll have to use the Metro.
Richard A BMW with only twelve thousand on the clock and it won't start. I ask you?
Hector Years ago I had a Morris Minor. D'you remember the Morris Minors? (*He looks round*) I suppose not. It was as good as gold.

He exits DR

Trevor Up for promotion, are you, Richard?
Richard Who told you that? (*He heads for the telephone and stops*)

Trevor and Sarah look at each other, embarrassed

(*Rounding on Sarah*) I see. (*He crosses to the telephone and dials a number*)

Sarah moves to the kitchen area to make coffee

You'd think a BMW would be reliable . . . I've been half an hour trying to get that car started.
Julie I'm going for an interview today, Richard.

Richard Great. (*He looks at the phone*) Where are they?
Sarah It's not nine yet.

Richard slams the phone down

Trevor I'm glad we've started the day with some spark. So often I sit here at breakfast and I yawn and the yawn goes right on until supper. I've high hopes for a day that's started so lively.
Richard (*moving to stand behind Trevor*) When we took you in we didn't know we had a waster on our hands.
Trevor I'm not a waster, I'm a thinker.
Richard You told us you were a chartered accountant.
Trevor I felt like a chartered accountant. I was wearing my brother's suit at the time. He's a chartered accountant.
Julie What I can't understand, Trevor, is this. You're obviously intelligent——
Trevor (*soothingly*) I know. Sticks out like a high forehead, don't it?
Richard You don't mind if I'm candid? I mean, you sit around all day listening to the clouds passing and cadging grub off my wife. I'm obliged to remind you that you pay for lodgings, not board and lodgings.
Sarah Trevor doesn't have much, Richard.
Trevor The occasional coffee.
Richard Half a leg of lamb. You should be out there, mate. Making your way. Doing it.
Trevor I don't subscribe to your ethos. I happen to think, you see, that the cabbage patch is being turned too often, and needs to lie fallow for awhile.
Richard How very trendy.
Julie (*reading*) The mass rapist has struck again.
Richard There's a surprise. Muggers, junkies, rapists play their home fixtures round here.
Sarah This was always a good address.
Richard So was Brixton.
Julie He's sick, that rapist. I really hope they find him soon.
Richard When they do, he'll probably turn out to be a facsimile of our bogus accountant.
Sarah (*quietly reproving*) Richard . . .
Richard Some waster. No job. No fixed abode. No purpose. A loner. Feeding on his fantasies—and other people.
Sarah Richard, you're being obnoxious—

Act I, Scene 1

Richard (*moving up to the telephone*) I'm phoning the firm again. One of us has to graft, pay taxes so the rest can loiter with intent.
Julie (*rising*) I'd better be going. Wish me luck.
Sarah Hope you get the job.
Julie Ta.
Richard Go for it, Julie. Remember, you can't begin to sail until you get on board.

Julie exits DL

(*Turning to Trevor*) I'd like a word in private with my wife. Perhaps you wouldn't mind using your own kitchen. You know the way. It's over there.
Trevor Of course. Certainly.

Trevor exits DR

Richard returns to the telephone

Richard Mr Bauer please. It's Richard. (*He points off* R; *to Sarah*) I'm not happy about that one.
Sarah (*crossing to the bureau*) He pays his rent.
Richard He's getting too familiar. (*Back on the phone. His tone becomes sycophantic*) Mr Bauer, it's Richard Higgs. I'm awfully sorry. My car's broken down . . . Pardon? . . . The timing mechanism, I think. . . . I won't be long. . . . Oh. . . . Right. Four o'clock then. . . . Once again, awfully sorry. . . . Thanks a million, Mr Bauer. (*He hangs up*) Appointment put back to four.
Sarah Was he annoyed?
Richard No. I'm seventy per cent up on target this year. (*He takes a notebook from his briefcase* RC) Can't argue with that.
Sarah Time for a coffee?
Richard Why not?

Sarah goes into the kitchen area

Sarah The adrenalin's flowing this morning.
Richard (*sitting in the armchair* R) This promotion means a lot to me, a lot to both of us. From tomorrow I should have executive status. It won't exactly be stamped across my forehead, but they'll all know. Well, I've planned for it; worked for it. Nothing's been left to chance.
Sarah Yes, you've been dedicated.

Richard And some.
Sarah I might even say . . . blinkered. (*She pours coffee*)
Richard That's the difference between us. Attitude: positive, negative.
Sarah Attraction of opposites.
Richard All the same, I want you to get to grips with this situation. You know what I'm on about.
Sarah What?
Richard I think we should sell——
Sarah No.
Richard Sarah——
Sarah (*emerging from the kitchen area*) No.
Richard (*sitting R of the table*) I don't . . . It's not the time to argue. Just back me with the lodgers, will you? That guy (*he points to the door* DR) is taking advantage.
Sarah Trevor's no trouble. (*She brings coffee to Richard*)
Richard He's sponging off you.
Sarah After he's paid the rent he doesn't have much left. Trevor's on his uppers. He doesn't own a thing. (*She collects her own coffee and sits at the kitchen table*)
Richard Not our problem.
Sarah The way you spoke to him about the rapist was disgraceful.
Richard I don't want to sound mercenary; but frankly . . . (*he takes out a pocket calculator*)

Sarah begins to smile

If we're going to feed and water them every day . . . (*He tots up on the calculator*) What are you smiling at? . . . I hate it when you smile like that. (*He makes notes*)
Sarah Sorry.
Richard We have to get our act together, Sarah.
Sarah Do what? (*She continues to smile during the following*)
Richard We're supposed to be in business. We don't have lodgers for fun. (*He tots up on his calculator*) I mean, I'm working day and night. (*Exasperated*) What are you smiling at?
Sarah Nothing.
Richard You know, if this promotion is confirmed today. If Bauer gives the nod, we have to start thinking about moving . . .
Sarah And starting a family.
Richard We'll need a better address first.
Sarah This was always a good address.

Act I, Scene 1

Richard The service bells stopped ringing years ago. Tradesmen don't call anymore . . . Now it's social workers. What *are* you smiling at?
Sarah Your pocket calculator. It's the most maddening sight. You, totting up the housekeeping on your pocket calculator.
Richard I need a calculator for work.
Sarah Leave it there.
Richard You're offended by this? (*He holds it up*)
Sarah Yes.
Richard All right. I'll eradicate it.
Sarah Please.
Richard You want me to eradicate? You want me to destroy my——
Sarah Pocket calculator. Yes!
Richard (*looking at the calculator*) It's solid silver . . . I won this. Two years ago. Top salesman. Remember? At the annual do. Park Lane Hotel. What a night. Unforgettable, wasn't it?
Sarah Oh yes. What was I wearing?
Richard What?
Sarah What was I wearing, Richard?
Richard No idea. Top man! (*He holds up the calculator*) Inscribed. Top man! I felt so warm, bathing in the glow of success, you know. Nothing like it. The evening superstar. (*He moves to the dining table*)
Sarah You'd better get to work.

Pause

Richard Does my promotion mean anything to you?
Sarah Let's not argue.
Richard I don't know . . . (*He sags*)
Sarah Of course it does!
Richard Look, if I am promoted our lives will change. You do understand that, darling. We'll have to entertain clients. Put on a bit of a show.
Sarah Be Mr and Mrs Up and Coming.
Richard Right. Right. At their new address in St. John's Wood, or Hampstead. Which would you prefer?

She turns away from him

I mean, given the choice. Mill Hill perhaps?

Sarah Look. You've had another go about moving; and I know there's some sense in what you say——
Richard We can't entertain with lodgers in the house. And guests don't care to visit no-go areas.
Sarah (*rising*) This is not a 'no-go' area!
Richard Not yet. Day by day this area declines. It's changed since Daddy's time. As for Grandad he'd——
Sarah You'll be late.
Richard Aren't you going to wish me luck?
Sarah As if you needed it.
Richard It helps.
Sarah Good luck, darling.
Richard I might be late.

They kiss

 Richard exits DL. *Trevor enters* DR

Trevor As one door closes another one opens.
Sarah You've been eavesdropping again.
Trevor True. I have to say, I picture you living somewhere else. In Salisbury or Winchester. Near a cathedral. You'd be having coffee mornings and bridge parties and your garden would be strewn with roses and honeysuckle. Mind if I have a slice of toast?
Sarah (*sitting* UL) Why not?
Trevor I haven't eaten since yesterday afternoon—— (*He moves to the kitchen alcove*)
Sarah Help yourself——
Trevor —when I had a bun.
Sarah Heavens above! Do you want egg and bacon?
Trevor No. No.
Sarah You must feed yourself properly!
Trevor A morsel of Welsh rarebit will do. I'll see to it.
Sarah This has got to stop, Trevor.
Trevor Would you like a nibble yourself?
Sarah It's causing too much friction between Richard and me.
Trevor Take just a minute to slip it under the grill.
Sarah If you worked you could——
Trevor When are you going to have a child?
Sarah Next year.
Trevor I just want to say this: if Richard falls down on the job you'll know where to come.

Act I, Scene 1								9

Sarah (*dryly*) Thank you . . .
Trevor Anytime.

Richard enters DL, *flustered*

Richard Took the wrong keys, didn't I?

Sarah moves to her bag. Richard looks suspiciously at the others

Back again, Trevor! You're a magpie. (*He looks sharply at Sarah*) What's going on? Eh?
Sarah (*handing him the keys*) Nothing's going on.
Richard Well it . . . (*He returns to the door and looks back at Trevor*) Watch it, you!

He exits DL

Trevor (*grinning*) You'd think he owns the place.
Sarah Actually, he doesn't. I inherited this house from my parents. I've lived all my life here.
Trevor Like a tree.
Sarah (*crossing to the bureau and picking up the photograph*) This is a family house, Trevor. Do you know what that means? The things we inherit are important to us. We become a trustee. I may own the house but I also owe it in some way. I've enjoyed so much happiness here.
Trevor It's not really a family house now, is it? Strangers have moved in.
Sarah You're not a stranger.
Trevor I am.
Sarah That's absurd.
Trevor I'm a stranger.
Sarah (*puzzled; looking at him*) This house hasn't changed, really. And the street is much the same. The trees have grown taller. The gardens are not as well kept but that's because there have been so many conversions. (*She sits* R *of the table*) All right, so I'm soppy about this house. I sit here and dream of the past and it's all too real. But when I open my eyes there's no sharp jolt of reality because I'm in my old home, with all the things I hold most dear, all around me.
Trevor Like a ghost house.
Sarah You sound like Richard.
Trevor He's a realist. I'll say that for him.

Sarah I wonder. Sometimes.

Trevor You're a dreamer. (*He crosses to the back door*) But you only have to open your back door . . .

He opens the back door to the muted, relentless throb of hard rock

. . . and you've got the rhythm of life.

Sarah Trevor——

Trevor —It's hard rock, Sarah.

Sarah Shut the door.

Trevor Punk rock. We can prattle all we like about inner city depravation. Who's to hear us?

Sarah (*roused*) That's *their* thing.

Trevor Today's rock! Dissonant! Crude! Angry! It's what's out there.

Sarah Shut the door!

Trevor Strobe lights away from Mantovani.

Sarah Will you please do as I say?

Trevor Richard does have a point, you see.

Sarah starts towards the door as if to close it herself

The underdog snaps. (*He closes the door*) Rockweiller! Can't really ignore it, you know . . . You can sit tight behind lace curtains, clad your house with insurance and your body with private health care. You can sing your own song . . . (*He crosses to the kitchen*) but who knows?

Sarah Knows what?

Trevor What calamities are in store . . . For instance . . . Sarah . . . Sarah, I do believe we're out of butter.

Punk music rises. Fade Lights to pre-set pattern

Scene 2

The same day, early evening

Trevor sits in the armchair DR *playing with a pocket chess set. The standard lamp is on*

A door slams off L. *Julie enters* DL *and sits in the other armchair. She*

Act I, Scene 2

grimaces as she removes her shoes. Trevor, intent on his game, pays her scant attention at first

Julie I didn't know such places still exist. The offices were up seven flights of stone steps in a warehouse. I was subjected to sexual harassment by an old duffer of sixty who ought to know better. . . . He stared at my legs. All through the interview. "Where are you working now, Miss Pringle?" He stared at my legs. "What have you done in the past?" Stared at my legs. "Have you any diplomas?" Stared at my legs. "Are you a touch typist?"

She looks at Trevor to elicit some response but he appears to be intent on his game

I didn't know what to do with them, my legs. I wanted to close them up, you know, like a telescope. I tell you, I couldn't get out of there fast enough. Nearly fell down the stone steps. Are you winning?

Trevor Losing.

This answer mystifies Julie, who pulls a face

What's the weather like?
Julie Nippy. How long you been playing chess?
Trevor Don't know . . . Lost count of the time.
Julie You must feel stifled being in all day.
Trevor Yes, I do. (*He moves a piece deliberately*)

Hector enters DR

Hector Hallo, Julie. Did you get the job?
Julie Didn't want it. No way. Next time that agency sends me for an interview I'm asking for danger money.
Trevor Shouldn't be so sexy.
Julie Pardon?
Trevor I said you shouldn't——
Julie —I get fed up with suggestive remarks, if you must know. I can't pass a building site for what they all jump up and down, gibbering like a bunch of baboons. Men are incredible. I get touched up on the tube and I got pinched rotten in Sorrento.
Trevor Well, you're safe with Hector and me. We don't go public with our peccadillos.
Julie (*to Hector*) What's he talking about?

Hector Richard's on to Sarah all the time, you know. About selling this house. Can you imagine that? A lovely house like this and he wants to sell it.
Julie Richard's very persuasive.
Hector But this is a family house.
Trevor It's a lodging house.
Julie Well, I don't care either way. (*She rises*) I worry more about that pigging rapist. Right now he could be doing the most ordinary things, just like any one of us; and then tonight, when it's dark, be out there, waiting to pounce . . . It makes my flesh creep . . . (*She shivers*)
Trevor Try not to think about it.
Julie Can't help myself.
Hector There aren't many places you can stay where there's family portraits on the wall. Memorabilia. Makes all the difference. I can't stand bare walls.
Trevor We don't belong here.
Hector I do.
Trevor Sarah belongs here. This house is full of memories for her.

Hector turns towards the door DL

Julie Where you going, Hector?
Hector To my room. I like to look out across the supermarket into the High Street. See them shutting up the shops. The workers hurrying home. Yes. There's always something to see.
Julie That's nice.
Hector My room is never dark. Lights from the supermarket. Lights from the High Street.
Julie Lonely though.
Hector No, no it's not.
Julie How did you come to end up here?
Hector Never you mind. You'll end up some place, some day. Strange as it may seem now.
Trevor (*crossing to the drinks trolley*) Fancy a drink? As soon as I feel the arteries begin to harden, when I can no longer do the trick, as the Irish say—that's my lot. I'll slip away with a bottle and a sharp razor, leaving only the memory of my perfect youth and ignoble intentions. Meanwhile . . .
Hector Meanwhile?
Trevor I'm becalmed. (*He stands* R *of the table*) You see, I come from

Act I, Scene 2   13

a respectable breed. My father is a surveyor. Vice captain of the golf club, stalwart of the Round Table. You can't be more entrenched than that. It's a life insurance made flesh. I left home. Goodbye comfort. Welcome adventure. Two years ago now. Drifted this way and that. Now I'm becalmed, waiting for another breeze. (*He offers Julie a drink*)

Hector You shouldn't touch that, Julie.

Trevor Be criminal to waste it. (*He pours Julie's measure into his own glass and gulps it down*)

Hector I can't stand by——

Trevor You're not turning supergrass? Better not, or I'll tell what I found in your room.

Hector You've been in my——?

Trevor Last week it was. Thursday, I think. Dull afternoon. Just like today. Nothing much to do.

Hector You entered my room?

Trevor The door wasn't locked, you see. It stood ajar. Well, we're all voyeurs in our quieter moments.

Hector (*moving closer to Trevor*) You actually went into my room uninvited?

Trevor I didn't take anything. I'm not a thief. Well, not so as you'd notice. I was just curious.

Hector You trespassed!

Trevor I only wanted to know you a little better.

Hector You trespassed!

Trevor I was looking for you, Hector.

Hector Liar! You knew I was out!

Trevor I was looking for you. The real you.

Hector That was unforgivable. What do you think, Julie?

Julie I think it's nice having a chat. Better than watching the telly. But you shouldn't have gone into his room, Trevor. You shouldn't really.

Trevor (*moving to the trolley to refill his glass*) How much do we know about each other? We live here as strangers. I thought there's got to be more to Hector. He isn't just an extension of the Hoover. A talking, walking, fact-finder. There's more to him than that. You bet your life. I found you, Hector, in your room. I discovered the inner man. In your chest of drawers. Under the shirts, with the vests and the long johns.

Hector You did what?

Trevor Yes. Cheers.
Hector You're evil, you are.
Trevor I do have an enquiring mind.

Hector, upset, moves back to the door DR

Hector! You can trust me. I want to be your friend.
Hector God spare me that.
Trevor I do really.
Hector You're not right, you're not.
Trevor Look at it this way, we now know each other better.
Hector You missed your vocation.
Trevor I could never be a copper——
Hector Should have been a sniffer dog.

He exits DR

Julie That was a rotten thing to do. Fancy going through his things. You haven't been down my drawers, have you?
Trevor Not yet.
Julie (*sitting at the dining table*) Well, I think you've behaved abysmally. Poor old Hector. He's really upset. What did you find in his room anyway?

Trevor stares at her

Well?
Trevor You sit there oblivious of your fantastic power.
Julie What?
Trevor Up there, on the landing, all that separates us is a bit of two by four. It's a false wall, and shouldn't come between us.
Julie What are you on about?
Trevor I can hear almost everything you do in that room upstairs. Your room, next to mine.
Julie (*aghast*) You listen to me?
Trevor Sometimes I feel I could walk right through the wall to get to you.
Julie You're weird, you are.
Trevor You don't know me, Julie. I have such . . . possibilities. (*He puts the whisky bottle back*) If I could redirect my life force there's no telling. But when I'm up there and I listen to you moving about, I'm overcome with hot flushes. All my spiritual guides wither before a giddy vision of you, sort of, centre spread, you know?

Act I, Scene 2   15

(*Apologetically*) I must admit that my sexual fantasies are pretty banal. I despise myself of course.

Julie So you should.

Trevor To find that I'm all of a tremble over flesh made fantasy.

Julie What?

Trevor But it's only human, isn't it? Nothing personal.

Julie You really are weird.

Trevor Natural enough.

Julie Sex don't do anything for me, I'm afraid. (*She rises to get her bag*)

Trevor No?

Julie Frankly, I can't see what all the fuss is about. I mean, it's supposed to be so tremendous. This . . . bloke . . . kept saying: "It's the most tremendous feeling in the world." So I thought I'd better try it. We pulled up outside a pub. I had a couple of brandies and Cokes first. Then we got in the car and went up a lane and did it. Afterwards, I thought, well really.

Trevor "Well really"?

Julie Yeah.

Trevor Well really . . . (*Recovering*) But you're right, in a way. There's much to be said for chastity, particularly these days. Caution certainly. I was hoping we'd have a chat. Get to know each other.

Julie looks at him scornfully and exits DL

Trevor stares at the door, nods and continues talking

Yes, have a pleasant talk. Converse. Like good fellows. (*He wanders across the room, looks at the small photograph of Sarah's father on the bureau and picks it up*) You see, Daddy, when I came away, all my friends were shacking up. Held fast by the ball and chain of wife and mortgage. Their main concerns are . . . economic. Well, everybody's on the make, you see. Precious little religion about—they pray to God as if he's a one-armed-bandit. Nobody listens! Nobody wants to think too deeply. Seems to me that as we tread through this wonderful world we can do one of two things: we can either look down and see the crap or keep our heads held high and tread in it!

Sarah (*off*) What's going on down there?

Julie (*off*) It's Trevor!

Trevor (*mumbling*) It's perdition . . .

Trevor exits hurriedly DR. *Sarah enters* DL. *She has changed into a smart outfit and looks ready to go out. She is closely followed by an agitated Julie. Sarah moves to the telephone table. Julie to* UR. *Sarah takes a pen from her handbag and sits* R *of the table to write a note*

Sarah I'm sorry, Julie, but I can't deal with it now.
Julie He says he listens to me.
Sarah That's absurd.
Julie He does. He has his ear against the wall.
Sarah I must leave a note for Richard.
Julie Can I change my room?
Sarah We haven't a spare.
Julie Can I change with Hector?
Sarah Hector won't change.
Julie If I can't I shall have to leave.
Sarah (*calling*) Hector! (*She knows that he is listening in the lodgers' kitchen*) Hector!

Hector enters with a carrier bag full of empty beer cans

Hector I'm not changing my room. No way!
Sarah (*patiently*) Now then——
Hector It's out of order to suggest such a thing.
Julie Trevor listens to me.
Hector I don't care. I mean, what would you think if you lived in a house and somebody knocked on the door and said: "We want to exchange. We want your house for ours?"
Sarah I do sympathize, Hector. It's just that Trevor's been getting on Julie's nerves.
Julie (*crossing to* L *of the table*) How would you like somebody listening to everything you do? (*Aghast*) Everything.
Hector I know what he's like. He went through my things.
Sarah He what?
Julie Yes, he did. When Hector was out.
Hector Invaded my room. Went through my drawers.
Sarah That's too much.
Julie You ought to get rid of him.
Hector I'm upset, I tell you. I am personally aggrieved. I can't handle any more hassle right now . . . I'm not changing my room. You've no right to ask such a thing. I've had that room for four years. It's

home to me. That room has my stamp on it. Everything is in order. All my stuff is within arm's reach. Precisely placed. There's no way I'm going to give that room up! It's mine and you're not having it! (*He moves to Julie, crossing behind the chairs and coffee table*)
Sarah All right. Nobody's changing rooms, Hector——
Hector People are always trying to take things from you. They won't leave you alone. Won't let you settle.
Sarah It's all right.

He breaks from Sarah to re-engage Julie

Hector I'm telling you, Julie. You can forget about that. No way are you moving in. So don't keep on about it. Got it?

He exits DL

Julie What's the matter with him? I only asked——
Sarah Oh dear. (*She moves to the coffee table, then on to the mirror*)
Julie —for a swop.
Sarah We mustn't upset Hector.
Julie Why not?
Sarah Just don't, that's all.
Julie Well, I'll have to think about things. I have to reconsider my position.

Sarah inspects her appearance in the mirror

You look great.
Sarah Thank you.
Julie Chic. You look really chic.
Sarah Honestly?
Julie I wouldn't lie about a thing like that.
Sarah (*turning back to the mirror to regard herself appreciatively*) How much is the bus fare into town?
Julie You're not going by bus?
Sarah (*moving to the window seat*) A number six takes me right there.
Julie It's a fair old stroll to the bus stop. (*She moves* L *of the coffee table*) And you don't walk around here after dark, Sarah. I never do. And you don't get on a bus or a tube late at night. Not on your own, you don't. Especially not dressed like that. No way.
Sarah I'm not used to being without a car.
Julie Catch a cab.
Sarah No, I've decided. (*She picks up a pen from the table*) I'm going

by bus. I'll be back in a couple of hours. Julie, I know I might seem biased, but, quite frankly, you won't find many lodgings as nice as this. Not at the price. (*She looks at her watch*) Heavens! I'm late. I haven't locked up or anything.

Julie Leave it to me.
Sarah Will you?
Julie Course.
Sarah You're a darling. I'll . . . I'll talk to Trevor tomorrow. (*She moves to the door* UL) See what I can do. Bye.
Julie Have a lovely time.

Sarah exits DL. *The front door bangs. Trevor enters* DR. *They stare at each other for a moment*

Stop gawking at me. I thought I made it plain, I don't like being stared at. (*She moves to lock up*)
Trevor (*reading Sarah's note*) Joined up writing. We have an intellectual in the house.
Julie It's for Richard. From Sarah. Tell him where she's gone.
Trevor Hector's out.
Julie Well?
Trevor And Richard's out. And Sarah's out. Everybody's out except us . . .
Julie (*starting to draw the curtains but turning back to Trevor*) I've got to lock up. You going to your room?
Trevor I really fancy you, Julie.
Julie I've told you——
Trevor What do I have to do, climb over the roof clutching a box of chocolates? You turn me on.

The curtain catches. She stands on a pouffe to reach the top. He puts his hand up to steady her

Julie Get off!
Trevor I've just giving you a hand.
Julie Keep your hands to yourself.
Trevor Where do you buy your lingerie, Marks and Spencer's?
Julie How do you know?
Trevor I've been given a sign by St Michael.

Julie hastily holds her skirt and climbs down. She moves DC

How about a dance? I bet you can't do ballroom dancing. You

Act I, Scene 2

ought to. It's a social grace. I learned by watching *Come Dancing* on the telly. The way those girls move. Could you move like that, Julie? Could you throw yourself into the rumba and then compose yourself for a genuflection afterwards? Genuflection restores a sense of propriety; no doubt about it. I think it would be a good idea if after sexual intercourse people honoured each other with a bow and a curtsy.

Julie (*stepping away from Trevor*) Really, I don't know what you're on about. A normal person wouldn't talk like that. I can't even understand half the words you use.

Trevor But you get my drift?

Julie (*mocking*) I think so.

Trevor (*moving* DR) It's a time for reappraisal. What with this, that and the other. Personally I don't want to take advantage of anyone. No way. That's not my style. I consider the other party. I'm not socially irresponsible. Look. (*He takes something from his pocket and holds it in his closed hand*)

Julie What is it? (*She steps close to him*)

Trevor Look. (*He approaches her*) Come on. You can trust me. Cross my heart and hope to die.

Julie leans forward to see what is in his hand. When he discreetly shows it to her she turns away sharply and moves L

Julie Do yourself a favour! Go and buy yourself a dirty raincoat!

Trevor I was just showing you that I'm a caring person.

Julie If I want somebody I'll be choosy and you'd be the last one!

Trevor You see, you're not just crumpet. You're what you might call, how can I say?—without being—you're—what's wrong with being a bit of crumpet? I'd feel flattered, if I was a bird. Even so. "Crumpet" is impersonal, I must admit. This is all about you and me; that's my point.

Julie "You and me" are words that don't go together as far as we're concerned. When I look twice at a fella I ask myself questions like, "Would I want to share his bathwater?" Well, I certainly wouldn't want to share yours.

Trevor That's a fine thing to say.

Julie You're unsavoury.

Trevor What's brought this on?

Julie I really think you don't know. That's the trouble.

Trevor (*holding her*) Can't we enjoy some fellow feeling, sip a little

companionship on the rocks? Surely, that's worth some effort?
Julie Take your hands off me.
Trevor Consider the alternative.
Julie Take your hands off me!
Trevor (*moving* UC) Don't get hysterical.
Julie I'm not.
Trevor We can talk things through. Slowly and gently.
Julie Inch by inch.

Pause

Trevor You're innately provocative. No need to add insults.
Julie No?
Trevor Calling me "unsavoury". . . That's not nice, Julie. That's not nice at all.
Julie (*sarcastically*) Oh dear.

She remains unabashed. Trevor moves away DC

Trevor Seems we're struggling.
Julie Struggling?
Trevor To find each other.
Julie Who needs to?
Trevor To talk even. You know, "talk"! You know, you open your mouth and——
Julie Who wants to?

Trevor moves back to Julie

Don't touch me!

He considers her

Trevor Shame.
Julie Good-night.

Trevor exits suddenly DL. *The front door bangs*

Julie turns off the main light, then moves back to the room and, after a moment's thought, picks up the telephone and dials a number

(*On the phone*) Melinda? It's Julie. . . . Hi . . . Just a quick word. . . . I'm on my landlord's phone. . . . Hold on a minute. (*She listens*)

There is a noise outside

Act I, Scene 3

Thought I heard a noise. . . . Yeah . . . Yeah . . . Listen. . . . (*She is distracted again when she thinks she hears a noise*) Yeah. . . . I'm still here . . . Listen. About tomorrow . . . Yeah. Right. Where? . . . OK. . . . I'm really looking forward to it. . . . Smashing. (*Distracted again, she turns away from the phone to listen*). . . . What? . . . Oh, I agree. . . . All right then. I can't wait. See you . . . Right. What? . . . That's amazing. . . . Yeah, I'm fine. . . . Bye, Melinda. (*She hangs up, looks round, tidies the chairs* R, *crosses to the kitchen and switches off the light. In the dark she moves* DL, *then remembers that she has not bolted the door* UR) The back door, stupid.

She crosses to the back door UR. *A faint light shows through the window*

The door swings open. The vague shadow of someone is seen momentarily in the doorway. Julie screams loudly

There is a resurgence of pop music against her screams

CURTAIN

SCENE 3

A few hours later

Sarah is on the telephone. Richard sits thoughtfully in the chair UL. *Hector is in the kitchen* UL. *Trevor sits* R *of the table. During Sarah's conversation, Hector moves closer to listen before returning into the kitchen area*

Sarah (*on the phone*) Hallo? I'm phoning about Miss Pringle who was admitted earlier this evening. Pardon? . . . I'm her landlady. . . . Can you tell me what's wrong? . . . How extensive are her injuries? . . . I see. Has she come round? . . . Quite . . . Quite. . . . Thank you. (*She hangs up*) They say her condition is serious but stable. (*She moves* C *and stands there thoughtfully*)

Richard Sit down, Sarah.

She continues to stare

   Sarah.

Sarah sits R of the table

She's all right then?
Sarah Her condition is serious.
Richard But stable, you said. That means they've got things under control, doesn't it?
Sarah I suppose so. I hope so.

Pause

Trevor Odd thing is you could see it coming. . . . I mean, she was so scared of being attacked. She worried about the rapist.
Hector Julie was, well, you know, conscious of herself. Yes.
Trevor An assault was almost wished upon her. Bound to happen.
Sarah (*firmly*) Nothing is bound to happen.

Richard rubs his forehead

Headache?
Richard I'd better take some tablets.
Sarah You shouldn't take tablets if you've been drinking.
Richard (*petulant*) I was celebrating.
Trevor Did you get the job?
Richard Yes.
Hector That's good news at least.
Richard I suppose so. I worked hard enough for it.
Hector Well-deserved promotion. Yes. (*He takes a glass to fetch water for Richard*)
Sarah You don't think it was the rapist who attacked Julie, do you?
Richard It was an opportunist burglar.
Trevor Is that what the police said?
Richard As good as.
Hector Ninety per cent of forced entries are done by opportunist burglars. Yes. (*He brings back the glass of water to Richard*)
Sarah But Julie was attacked.
Richard Well, she disturbed him . . .
Hector Your gentleman burglar is a fiction of the past.
Richard Quite. He now bashes up the occupant or vandalizes the property. It's his idea of a fringe benefit.
Trevor An atavistic reminder.
Richard What?
Trevor Never feel too secure.

Act I, Scene 3   23

Richard Who does?
Trevor The winners.
Richard When Julie was attacked there was no winner. Both villain and the victim were losers.
Trevor There's a thought.
Richard What has he achieved?
Trevor He made his mark.
Richard Rubbish.
Trevor Announced his presence among the masses. You have to take notice of me, he says.
Richard Christ . . . .
Sarah Shut up! Please.

Richard leaves the glass on the table and sits R *of the table*

What I can't understand is, the police were here for such a short time.
Richard It wasn't a big deal around here.
Sarah That's disgraceful.
Richard You heard what that copper said: "The payload's heavy tonight." Here there's no time to solve crimes. They have their work cut out just logging them.
Hector (*moving* UR) They'll return though.
Richard You reckon?
Hector Yes, they'll return. Didn't they question you, Sarah?
Sarah Briefly.
Hector And you, Trevor?
Trevor No. I slipped out.
Hector They'll be back then.

He exits DL

Richard They questioned the rest of us.
Sarah In a perfunctory way.
Richard It's a perfunctory crime.
Sarah Julie's in intensive care, for heaven's sake! (*She moves* R)
Richard (*rising*) It's late. Well past bedtime. (*He crosses to collect his cigarettes* DR)
Trevor I'm a night bird myself.
Sarah What do you do? At night?
Trevor Come down and make a coffee . . . (*he looks at Richard*) from

Sarah   my own jar of Gold Blend, of course . . . Sometimes I read, play chess.
Sarah   I've never heard you.
Trevor   Chess is a quiet game. Sometimes, I just sit here. Or I stand in the doorway, with the lights off and bask in the shadows.
Richard   You what?
Trevor   It's my form of toning up. Sunbathing for the skin. Shadows for the soul. Every house has its own smell. Its own stories to tell. They're found in the shadows.
Sarah   (*to Trevor*) What does this house tell you?
Richard   Don't encourage him.
Trevor   It's a family house. If I listen intently I can hear your laughter when you were a child.
Richard   Oh yeah?
Trevor   And I hear your daddy saying: "I'm entrusting this house to you, Sarah."
Richard   You've been ear-wigging!
Trevor   "And I don't want you to sell it."
Richard   (*rising*) Mind your own bloody business!
Trevor   Can't make sense of business or much else really. How is it that we return to this happy home and find Julie staining the carpet? Is nothing sacrosanct? Not even a family house?
Richard   What would you know about family houses?
Trevor   Only what Sarah's told me.
Richard   Anyway, "family house", what does that mean? This is a house. Full stop. When we leave, it reverts to a shell, nothing else.
Sarah   I don't believe that. A family has invested this house with its lives.
Richard   One day, new owners will decorate and refurbish. They might rip out the old wiring, replace the roof tiles, put in new windows. All too soon it'll be unrecognizable.
Sarah   Never. Not to me.
Richard   What do we leave behind then? Ghosts? Sensations? A mysterious, intangible, indelible reminder of ourselves? Where? In the walls? Under the beds? In the atmosphere?
Sarah   Who knows?
Richard   It's absurd.

The doorbell rings

Who's that? (*As he goes, mumbling*) At this time of night.

Act I, Scene 3   25

He exits DL

Trevor How you feeling?
Sarah All right.
Hector Try not to worry about it.
Trevor Could have happened anywhere.

There are voices off stage

> *WPS Hammond enters* DL, *followed by Richard. She is trim, smart and brisk. She stands* L *of* C

Sarah is R *of* C. *Trevor remains sitting* DR. *Richard moves* UR

Hammond Sorry to disturb you at such a late hour, Mr Higgs. I saw the light on. I was asked to look in, if you were still up.
Richard That's all right.
Hammond Apparently, we have statements from everyone but . . . Mr Billingham.
Trevor I'm Mr Billingham.
Hammond I'm WPS Hammond.
Trevor Are you sure?
Hammond This is just routine.
Trevor (*ironically*) For you.
Richard If you don't need me, I'll go to bed.
Hammond That's fine, thank you.
Richard Good-night.

He exits DL

Sarah Would you like me to go?
Hammond Doesn't matter. Now then, Mr Billingham——
Trevor (*abruptly*) Yes?

Hammond takes out her notebook. Sarah sits at the table UL

Hammond You're a touch bristly.
Trevor Past my bedtime.
Hammond Where were you this evening?
Trevor At the Albert Memorial.
Hammond Were you alone?
Trevor One is never alone at the Albert Memorial.
Hammond Really? What were you doing there?
Trevor I was trying to reconcile Queen Victoria's devotion to the

Consort with her passion for whoopee cushions. Excuse me, but I didn't expect a female.

Hammond The Chief Superintendent would have come personally but he's tied up just now.

Trevor Down at the Masonic Lodge, is he?

Hammond Look. I'm just filling in——

Trevor —your overtime sheet?

Hammond (*moving* R) What time did you leave here?

Trevor Just after Sarah.

Hammond Were you the last one to be in the house with Miss Pringle?

Trevor Must have been. We had a chat. In here. Just a chin wag. Usual trivia. You know the sort of thing. Cost of living. The F.T. index, summits, famines, pestilence and death. All covered in less time than it takes to watch the six o'clock news.

Hammond I see.

Trevor Do you?

Hammond Is there anything else?

Trevor Not really.

Hammond Nothing at all?

Trevor Well, I don't know. Are you treating the matter seriously; or will it just be written off as an everyday story of urban blight?

Hammond We're treating the matter seriously, Mr Billingham.

Trevor Good. Nice to see you on the job. (*He grins*) I thought coppers spent most of their time in the pub calling each other "guv".

Hammond Were you on intimate terms with Julie?

Trevor No such luck.

Hammond Did you get the impression that she was expecting a visitor? (*She moves* C)

Trevor No.

Hammond How did she seem to you?

Trevor Her usual self.

Hammond Mrs Higgs, do you get references for your lodgers?

Sarah Usually. Yes. (*Firmly*) Yes.

Hammond I hope you check them carefully. They can be faked.

Trevor Mine was.

Sarah Sergeant, who do you think did it?

Trevor One thing's for sure—the butler didn't.

Hammond Most burglaries are committed by the opportunist. In and out in five minutes. Nick the telly. Nick the video.

Sarah But nothing was taken.
Hammond No. (*She crosses to the door*) Sorry if I've kept you up, Mrs Higgs. Don't bother to see me out. Good-night.
Sarah Good-night.
Hammond (*with an afterthought; stopping at the door*) What do you do for a living, Mr Billingham?
Trevor Nothing.
Hammond I see.

Hammond exits

Sarah turns on Trevor

Sarah You don't help yourself, do you?
Trevor To do what?
Sarah Anything. You deliberately antagonized that policewoman. Now if there's half a chance of nobbling you for the crime, I'm sure she'll do it. And who could blame her?
Trevor (*ironically*) How can you, a respectable householder, think such a thing?
Sarah Give over, Trevor. (*She looks at the spot where Julie fell*)
Trevor The attack's unnerved you, hasn't it?
Sarah A bit.

Hector looks in DL

Hector Who was that?
Trevor The police.
Hector What did they want?
Sarah It was just routine, Hector. Nothing to worry about. Tomorrow I want to clean up this room. I wondered if you'd care to give me a hand?
Hector Only too ready. We'll have a good clean up, Sarah. Yes.
Sarah Thank you——
Hector —you can leave it to me, if you like. I'll get up at cock-crow. I never sleep much after five anyway. Before you come down to breakfast I'll have gone over the place. Tell-tale traces will have disappeared and it'll all be right as rain. You'll see. (*He stares at the floor where Julie fell*) Is that Julie's blood? That is blood, isn't it?
Sarah Yes, Hector.
Hector It's dried out now. Best thing to do is to rinse it off first and then we'll use a carpet shampoo. That should do the trick. That

won't give us much bother. (*He rubs his foot in it*) Well, we've got to pull ourselves round, haven't we?
Sarah Indeed, we have.
Hector Get back to normal.
Sarah Quite.
Hector I was thinking about China this afternoon.

Trevor groans

Yes. China. Do you know that in China they have a Palace of Earthly Tranquillity, The Hall Where The Heart Is . . . Yes.
Sarah "The Hall Where . . ." Excuse me, Hector.

She exits DL

Hector And The Palace Of Vigorous Old Age. They know that a place has its own spirit, you see . . . Have you said anything about my business? You know, what you found out about me.
Trevor No.
Hector I suppose you will.
Trevor No.
Hector Can I trust you, Trevor?
Trevor That's up to you.
Hector The coppers will rake it up, of course. When you've got form you're prime.
Trevor What do you make of this attack on Julie?
Hector What can you say? In London a house or a flat is broken into every three minutes of every day. Yes.
Trevor And back in the thirties, it was considered to be unbridled licence when the King and Mrs Simpson were seen pruning roses in their pyjamas. I remember you telling me that.
Hector Did I? (*He moves to the door* DR)
Trevor That's how I'll remember you, Hector. As a fund of information . . . You're encyclopaedic.
Hector Those newspaper clippings, the ones you found in my room, I've just burnt them.
Trevor Good.
Hector Sent my past up in flames.

He exits DR

Trevor Best way. (*He rises and stares at the spot where Julie fell. He looks across to the door as if measuring the distance*)

Act I, Scene 3

Sarah enters DL

Sarah What did Hector have to say?

Trevor Not a lot. Thought you'd gone to bed.

Sarah I wouldn't sleep if I did. I feel drained but somehow not tired. You know how it is. Besides, I have to speak to you . . . It's about Julie. She wanted to change her room. She said she'd leave if she couldn't.

Trevor Any chance of a drink?

Sarah Help yourself.

Trevor I've become rather partial to whisky since I've been here.

Sarah So I've noticed. (*She sits at the bottom of the table*)

Trevor You know, you're an odd pair, you and Richard. You're there together, but like figures in a Swiss clock. He turns one way, you the other.

Sarah At least he knows what he wants.

Trevor More. That's what he wants. Just like the rest. More.

Sarah He has his role to play. You're still trying to invent yourself.

Trevor What do you know about me? Or any of us? About Julie or her attacker?

Sarah Julie wanted to leave because of you.

Trevor I shouldn't pay much attention to that. (*He moved* R *of the table*) There was a guy I met once on a train coming back from Norwich. We had a great chin-wag; but he stopped me when I'd been waxing metaphysical. He tapped me on the knee, leaned close and said: "Tell me your truth and I'll tell you mine."

Sarah Did he really say that?

Trevor Yes.

Sarah How odd.

Trevor Truth can be "odd" . . . disconcerting. Most of us fear to give it the time of day; but it's now late at night. The hour for truth.

Sarah Julie wanted to leave because she felt threatened by you.

Trevor That's why I stay up late. It's easier to think clearly, more truthfully. I'm glad to have this chance . . . (*he spreads his hands*) You know.

Sarah I'm very ordinary, Trevor.

Trevor shakes his head

I am as you see me, you know. I wish I could be more outgoing. I wish I could say "F" and "B" and put my underclothes out to dry on the washing line . . . Sometimes, I wish I had a hidden vice. Something to make me . . . interesting.

Trevor That's easily done.

Sarah Not with me it isn't.

Trevor What really counts with you?

Sarah I'm not sure.

Trevor Think about it. You know how it is when you should have made love to someone. You didn't and you never get another chance. This is a moment of truth and the chance may not come our way again.

Pause

Sarah I'm not sure . . . Well, Richard matters, of course——

Trevor —of course.

Sarah And my home.

Trevor (*looking at the portrait*) And Daddy. Alive or dead.

Sarah Did you tell the man on the train your truth?

Trevor I didn't know what to say. So I got up and opened the window.

Pause

Sarah Julie wanted to leave here because of you.

Trevor She's paranoid. (*He confronts her across the table*) My mum used to make the most marvellous marmalade sponge. The marmalade used to be in the bottom of the basin. Then when it was cooked she'd turn the basin upside down and hot marmalade would trickle down the side of the sponge and steam would rise. It was like an orgasm . . . I don't suppose you've had any marmalade sponge lately?

Sarah You'd upset Julie. Frightened her.

Trevor (*firmly*) I am not responsible, Sarah.

Sarah (*ironically*) How nice. Just like being a child again. Nothing to worry about. Leave everything to the grown-ups. I have my Dinky toys and my spaceman's helmet, and if I'm very good, when I grow up, the Fairy Godmother—Social Security—will keep giving me benefits.

Trevor We all have our dreams.

Sarah (*resigned*) Yes.

Trevor Don't we just. (*He stares at her*)

Pause

Act I, Scene 3

Sarah As a girl I had everything. My world was complete. It seemed inevitable that things would fall into place, that happiness was ordained. Daddy was wonderful. Then Daddy died. In his place I got Richard, and Richard brought in lodgers. The lodgers have brought us to this . . . That bus ride was a nightmare. I couldn't walk because I might be mugged or raped——
Trevor You're as bad as Julie. Paranoid.
Sarah Poor Julie.
Trevor I'm more than a bit peckish, Sarah. (*He moves into the kitchen*)
Sarah There's food in the larder.

Trevor looks back questioningly

It's all right. Richard goes to sleep as soon as his head hits the pillow.

Trevor moves L behind Sarah's back. He returns with bread and a knife. He examines the knife

What's the matter . . .? Trevor?

Pause

Trevor You wanted my truth. I'm a bit manic-depressive, actually. Not much. Just a teeny bit. Off and on. Spend too much time alone, I suppose. Don't have the gift of friendship. Winston Churchill was a touch manic-depressive. Couldn't bear to lean against the side of a boat, or stand on a platform before an approaching train. He was wary of the compulsion to jump, you see. I'm nervous of dangerous implements, myself. Like a knife. (*He leans forward and holds the knife close to her throat*) Here it is. In my hand. Wouldn't take much, would it? Not much at all. The merest slip. A quick lunge. All over in a second . . . Bet you'd love to move, wouldn't you? Get off that chair. Walk away. Perhaps you trust me, even if Julie didn't. No. No. (*He moves away*) It's the head girl seeing it through. You were the head girl, weren't you? Weren't you?
Sarah Yes.
Trevor Of course. Well done. You've earned yourself a slice of bread. (*He tosses the bread on to the table and holds the knife between them*)
Sarah You don't scare me, Trevor.
Trevor You miss the point. I scare myself.
Sarah (*rising*) Why?

Trevor Compulsion.
Sarah Are you serious? Because if you are, that really is frightening.
Trevor Now you're nervous.
Sarah You really thought you might use the knife on me?
Trevor It was a possibility.
Sarah Why?
Trevor You were so vulnerable.
Sarah That's horrible.
Trevor Scared me to death.
Sarah What stopped you . . .? Trevor . . .? Common sense stopped you . . . You really are scared?
Trevor Out of my wits.
Sarah (*closing on him*) Of what you might do to me?
Trevor Yes.

They stare at each other. Then Trevor looks away. Sarah takes the knife and holds it out to him, standing close

Sarah Take it.
Trevor No thanks.
Sarah Handle it.
Trevor No.
Sarah Put the knife in your hand and point it at me.
Trevor Don't want to.
Sarah I dare you.

He takes the knife from her

Well . . .? Well?
Trevor Why are you doing this?
Sarah It's the first really crazy thing I've ever done.
Trevor Could be the last.
Sarah Now that is frightening.
Trevor Sarah . . . (*He leans threateningly forward but stops as the door opens*)

Richard enters DL

Richard What's going on!? D'you know what the time is?

Trevor breaks L *to the alcove*

What are you talking about?
Sarah Nothing much. I'll be up in a minute. I can't sleep. (*She sits* UL)

Act I, Scene 3

Richard It's . . . late enough.
Sarah (*sarcastically*) I've been upset. What happened earlier, you know?

Pause

Richard We ought to send some flowers to the hospital in the morning. Will you see to it?
Sarah Yes. Of course.
Richard Right then . . .
Sarah Did you know Julie intended leaving?
Richard No. Did she say why? (*He moves forward to* C)

Sarah looks awkwardly at Trevor. Following her gaze, Richard turns to Trevor

Do you know. . . . Well?
Trevor Probably off to take the air in Patagonia. Could be going for a stroll in the Hindu Kush. (*He sits in the chair* DR) Anywhere's safer than civilization, Richard.
Richard (*to Sarah*) Are you coming up to bed? Or are you going to sit here all night?
Sarah I'll just have a coffee first. (*She moves towards the kitchen*)
Richard Don't be long then.

He exits DL

Sarah I believe you tormented Julie for something to do. Look, Trevor, if you had a job you wouldn't have the time for such nonsense. That sounds trite, I know, but I'm worried about you. You'll end up in trouble, I know it. Let me help you. Please. Let me help you. I want to. (*She joins him*)
Trevor Be a friend.
Sarah Yes.
Trevor That'd be nice.
Sarah You haven't any friends, have you?
Trevor Had one once. A true friend. Joe. He was a middle-aged advertisement salesman on the local paper. On the face of it he was as regular as a season ticket. In his youth he wanted to be a writer and to travel the world. He never got started, nowhere near it. Instead of being a literary lion of London and Paris he found himself a family man in Upminster . . . So he smothered his ideal in the nine to five. And he read. Reading was his consolation. Until

one morning he shot himself. Nobody could understand why. He had a steady job. Nice wife and kids. The mortgage was just about paid for. He left no letter. Nobody knew why he shot himself. But I did. I knew it was the nearest he could get to being Ernest Hemingway.
Sarah Was that meant to tell me something about you?
Trevor Maybe. (*He moves towards the door* UR) Life seems more dramatic at night, doesn't it? Did you know we're supposed to be at our lowest ebb at three a.m.?
Sarah Is that when your friend committed suicide?
Trevor It was six-thirty on a May morning. It had rained overnight. The birds were singing. Joe went out to the shed. He wasn't the type to make a mess on the carpet.
Sarah Poor man. Poor wife and kids.

Trevor moves towards her and holds out his hands

No, Trevor.
Trevor Take my hands. Trust me. Julie didn't.
Sarah She didn't?
Trevor Trust me. That's all I ask.

Sarah crosses to him and takes his hands

Sarah Who attacked Julie?
Trevor Would it scare you stiff if you were holding his hands?
Sarah We've still got our late night honesty pact, have we?
Trevor That's why I asked the question.
Sarah Did you?
Trevor I wanted to have my wicked way with her.
Sarah Did you?
Trevor Oh yes. (*He grins*)

The telephone rings

I wanted . . . (*He is distracted by the telephone*) This late it must be a heavy breather.
Sarah Might be the hospital.

He releases her hands

(*She moves up to the telephone*) I don't understand you. I like to make sense of things. You're not what you seem. (*She is distracted by the phone and turns to the receiver*) Hallo? . . . Yes. . . . Who is

that? . . . Really? Who's speaking? . . . I see. . . . Why don't you go to the police? . . . (*She hangs up*)
Trevor Who was it . . .? Sarah?
Sarah A guy from next door.
Trevor What did he say?
Sarah Nothing. Nothing much. (*She turns away, looking worried*)
Trevor Tell me.

Pause

Sarah He said one of us attacked Julie. He saw the unmistakable figure in the garden.

Trevor turns and quickly opens the back door

There is a quiet throb of hard rock from next door

CURTAIN

ACT II

Scene 1

Saturday morning of the following week

Sarah is in the kitchen. Richard is on the telephone

Richard We'd ensure vacant possession, of course. . . . All right. All right. Don't give me the negatives. Just give me the good news. . . . How much? (*He writes down a figure*) Thank you. We'll get back to you. (*He hangs up and places the notepaper before Sarah*) Let's not prejudge the price . . . He thinks that a prospective buyer may convert this house into two, maybe three flats.

Sarah looks sick at this prospect

You're never going to feel the same, you know.
Sarah It's not just what happened to Julie.
Richard Well, at least she's recovering. It's you I'm worried about now. Whoever attacked Julie could return. He or someone like him . . . Sarah? There always comes the day when you have to face the audit.

She hands the pad back to him. She is nervous, thoughtful

What's the matter?
Sarah What do you think?
Richard You've got to try to erase what happened here . . . You must. Please.
Sarah I know.
Richard Get back to reality. Remember the good times.
Sarah When we met.
Richard The Young Conservatives Club.
Sarah Saturday night dance.
Richard My first visit.
Sarah You weren't even a Conservative.

Act II, Scene 1

Richard I became one. Overnight.
Sarah You were so intense; that's what attracted me.
Richard I thought I was desperately charming. "Desperate" is the word. I'd have stood on my head to please you . . . I'd seen you before, of course. At the tennis club.
Sarah That's news.
Richard That's why I really joined the Conservatives.
Sarah So you planned our meeting?
Richard I plan everything.
Sarah Well, well. All our little secrets leak out sooner or later. I suppose. But then I never was very alert.
Richard True. You don't know what's going on half the time.
Sarah I've realized how little I know of life around here. I don't even shop locally.
Richard I was thinking of us. Anyway why should you "shop locally"?
Sarah Because . . . (*She moves from behind the table*) if you don't, you can lose touch: with neighbours, events, social changes, what's acceptable and what isn't. It seems that we should accept a burglary or an assault as . . . routine. I'm now told this sort of thing happens all the time.
Richard You're a bit naïve, darling.
Sarah Perhaps.
Richard Unworldly.
Sarah Yes.
Richard It's all right——
Sarah It isn't. It seems as if I've been in purdah for the last two or three years. I have to get out more, make new friends.
Richard If we lived in a better area——
Sarah It has nothing to do with the house. Since I gave up my job I've been trapped.
Richard Looking after the lame ducks.
Sarah Maybe. When I was at the bus stop that night, only a couple of us bothered to queue. When the bus arrived the rest fell on it. I was in a scrum of hacking elbows and feet. I was barged on board and launched upstairs. A woman puffed away in the non-smoking area.
Richard You shouldn't have gone——
Sarah —Two yobbos had a radio going full blast——
Richard —You should have taken a cab——
Sarah —I politely asked the woman to put her fag out, and got a

mouthful. After I left the bus I found my brooch had gone.
Richard That's just about par for the course around here.
Sarah You've never really regarded this house as a home, have you?
Richard It isn't mine, is it?
Sarah It's ours.
Richard No.

Hector enters DL. *He carries a small package in his hand*

Hector A little prezzie. (*He proffers the package*) Roman Bath Oils from Harrods . . . Went in there out of the rain. Nice and warm in Harrods.
Sarah You shouldn't. (*She takes the package and sits* L *of the coffee table*)
Hector Read what it says on the label: "Fit for the gods. It is for those who live in centrally heated homes where dehydration of the skin leads to premature ageing." Yes. Not thinking of selling, are you? You're not thinking of packing old Hector off into a cardboard box in Lincoln's Inn Fields? Not after all this time.

Sarah places the bath oils on the coffee table

Richard The break-in really upset Sarah, you know.
Hector (*sulkily*) The coppers aren't bothered about it. Wasn't even reported in the local rag.
Richard Somebody broke into her home. Even if nobody was assaulted that can be very upsetting for a woman, you know. Even make her want to sell up.
Sarah Oh yes?
Richard (*reprovingly*) Darling . . .
Sarah Just a thought.
Richard (*to Hector*) Anyway, we've been thinking about leaving . . . from time to time. If we should decide to pack up, we'll give you plenty of notice.
Hector I don't need notice. I want to be settled. Thought I was. Of course, I know you want the place to yourselves; that's natural enough. I understand.
Sarah Hector——
Hector This place has been like home for me. Yes. You've made me happy, feel like one of the family. Not that I want to intrude. No, never let it be said. You'll find you won't even notice me about the place. I'll be invisible. Yes. (*He turns from one to the other*) "Good

heavens," you'll say. "Who was that?" "That was Hector," you'll say. "Hector? Oh, old Hector." . . . (*He smiles*) Yes . . . Yes. . . . I promise. (*He looks winsomely from one to the other*) Besides, I'm getting old. I don't suppose I shall drag on forever.

Richard Listen . . . Sarah's upset. You know she had a phone call, don't you? Suggesting that someone here attacked Julie.

Hector You think it might be me?

Richard Not necessarily.

Hector (*alarmed*) Sarah?

Sarah I don't think it was you. Honestly.

Hector I swear. I swear, Sarah.

Sarah Hector——

Richard It makes us uncertain about having lodgers, you see. Without lodgers the house is too big for us. Besides, it's obvious that when we start a family, we'll want to rear our children in a more, shall we say, salubrious area. (*He turns away*)

Hector Right. "Salubrious". Yes. (*He moves* R) This could still be a nice place to live. But if respectable people desert it, how can it be? All you're doing is handing it over to "them".

Richard "Them" are already here.

Hector What do you mean?

Richard This area's terminally knackered. What did you think I meant?

Hector Never mind.

Hector exits DL, *meeting Trevor at the door as he enters*

Trevor What's the matter with Hector?

Richard We've just told him we might be moving. Now you know.

Sarah It's not at all certain yet, Trevor, and, of course, we'll give you plenty of notice.

Trevor Sure. Thanks. Just palm me off with a couple of grand and I'll go quietly.

Richard You can get stuffed.

Trevor Only kidding, Richard.

Richard I should think so.

Trevor Make it five grand.

Richard Get lost!

Richard exits UR. *There is punk rock music heard from the neighbours as he goes out*

Trevor You look fed up . . . worried. (*He stands L of the kitchen table*)

Sarah I am. I still don't want to sell the house. And there's something else.

Trevor (*turning towards the kitchen*) I told you my secrets.

Sarah All of them?

Trevor Of course not.

Sarah (*revealing some anxiety; looking around*) I've got a problem with Hector. You see, I've never told Richard the truth about him. And now I feel I should. A few days before Hector arrived here as a lodger, a woman from the probation service called and asked me would I be prepared to take him. She warned me that he had just been released from prison after serving fifteen years. She said he was reformed and could be trusted. I felt sorry for him. I didn't say anything to Richard because I knew he would be outraged at the idea and never agree to it.

Trevor So?

Sarah Hector's proved himself to be a model lodger.

Trevor Sure he has.

Sarah But now this nasty business has hit us and I'm, well, confused. Oh, I don't believe Hector has anything more to do with the attack than you have. I mean, how could he? Why would he? It's absurd . . . illogical. But I keep thinking about that phone call . . . That's why I'm letting Richard enquire about selling the house . . . I feel uncertain here now . . . I simply don't know . . . I seem to be losing control. I've always been . . . so . . . sure . . . of myself.

She sits at the kitchen table. Trevor strokes her hair

Trevor You know what Hector did?

Sarah Of course. The woman told me. And later Hector himself.

Trevor He killed his sister. He stabbed her to death, didn't he?

Sarah How do you know?

Trevor I found newspaper cuttings in a drawer in his room. I looked in one day, you see. The drawer was open and lying there inside were these cuttings. I think it's what triggered my knife phobia.

Richard enters UR

Trevor breaks away to behind the table

Richard What are you two up to?

Sarah looks to Trevor for guidance

Act II, Scene 1   41

Trevor Tell him . . . Might as well.
Sarah It's about Hector. He has a criminal record.
Richard What?
Sarah He murdered his sister.

Pause

Richard When did you find out?
Sarah I've known all along. Ever since he came. The probationary service told me. I'm sorry, Richard, I should have told you.
Richard (*with mounting anger*) Yes, you should have . . . Yes, you most certainly . . . For chrissake! You should have told me that!
Sarah He swore to me that he could never kill again, or do anything violent.
Richard I bet he did. (*He looks at Sarah and shakes his head*) No wonder those animals next door told you that someone here had done for Julie. I can't believe that you——
Sarah I don't think he did it.
Richard Oh no! Most unlikely! Coppers? You'd think they'd have been on to him. A murderer!
Trevor Hold on.
Richard Berks! They've defaulted badly on this one. Hector's going to have to go. Today.
Trevor You think he attacked Julie?
Richard With his record? (*He moves* DR. *Scornfully*) Oh no.
Trevor Give him a break.
Richard I'll give him the boot.
Trevor (*moving round the foot of the table*) Richard. You must do lots of sums in your job. Estimates, costings, prices. I wonder how you've been managing this last week. (*He takes a calculator from his pocket*) Catch!
Richard (*examining the calculator*) How long have you had it?
Trevor Since the night Julie was attacked. It is yours, isn't it? (*He sits at the foot of the dining table*)

Sarah crosses quickly to look at the calculator

Sarah Richard?
Trevor I found it out there. On the night of the attack.
Sarah Where?
Trevor In the garden.
Sarah Richard . . . for heaven's sake.

Richard You're really hacking away at it, aren't you? Both of you. Your faith in me is touching, darling. What are you thinking? That I really did plan a break-in to force you to sell up? (*He turns aside for a moment, exasperated*) Don't you remember!? You asked me to throw this. Well, I went out the back to get your car from the garage. I knew we were still at odds and that aggravated me. I felt in my pocket—for the car keys, and pulled out the calculator. My precious little calculator which stood between us, or so it seemed. Crazy! Stupid! But that's how it read. So I chucked it! Did as you asked! Angrily, I chucked it away in the garden! I didn't even look to see where. Did as you asked ... (*Annoyed*) Besides, what possible motive could I have for attacking Julie?
Sarah What motive has anybody here?
Richard With a nutter in the house, who needs a motive?
Trevor It was just an assault.
Richard Right. It was just an assault, a burglary gone wrong. But now my wife tells me we have a lodger who killed his sister, that all this time I've been harbouring a bloody murderer, for chrissake.

The doorbell rings

Richard exits to answer it

Sarah Why didn't you tell me you found that calculator?
Trevor Would you have wanted to know?
Sarah Why not? I knew there would be a simple explanation.
Trevor I didn't.

WPS Hammond and Richard enter. Hammong crosses UC

Hammond Sorry to intrude again. I've called to tell you that Julie's discharged herself from hospital.
Richard (*to the others*) She must be OK now if she's left.
Hammond She discharged *herself*.
Richard Well, I suppose, that's her prerogative.
Hammond The hospital rang us because they're concerned about her condition.
Trevor What's wrong with her?
Hammond They're not sure, yet. I thought she'd be here.
Sarah She's bound to come back. Her things are here. (*To Hammond*) Would you like a coffee?

Act II, Scene 1

Hammond Thank you.

Sarah goes into the kitchen UL *to make the coffee. WPS Hammond walks thoughtfully across the room and opens the back door. There is the noise of punk rock. After a few seconds she closes the door*

    Noisy neighbours.
Richard Barbarians.
Hammond Have you asked them to turn it down?
Sarah By letter and by word of mouth.
Richard They replied by word of mouth.
Hammond There's a noise abatement officer at the town hall.
Richard Works on Saturdays. That's the one night we get some peace. They're smart, you see. Next door. Underprivileged but streetwise. Housing benefit and two grand's worth of hi-fi.
Sarah Why won't the police help?
Hammond It's not our job. Sorry. If we had a valid reason to call—if for instance drugs were being used—we might be able to do something. I suppose I could have a word with them.
Richard It'll be a waste of time.
Trevor Any leads?
Richard The bobby on the beat said it was the work of an opportunist burglar.
Hammond Did he?
Richard "Almost certainly", he said.

Pause

Sarah You must need a thick skin to do your job. I couldn't do it.
Trevor Why do *you*?
Hammond My father was a copper and my grandfather before him.
Trevor Ah. It's congenital, eh?
Hammond And I wanted to do something to make this a better world for my kids to grow up in.

Sarah brings the coffee across. The uneasy situation is now heightened when the front door bangs

    Julie enters carrying her bag. She looks drawn and ill

Hammond Hallo, luv.

Julie looks moodily at them

    How are you feeling?

Julie All right.
Hammond You look tired.
Sarah We didn't expect you out so soon.
Julie Shortage of beds.
Hammond Really?
Sarah The sister told me you'd be in for at least another week.
Julie Shortage of beds.
Sarah Sit down, Julie. You must be tired.
Julie Yes, I am.
Sarah Trevor, take her case up.

Trevor moves below the table

Julie No.
Sarah You mustn't carry it yourself.
Julie I don't want him to touch my things.
Hammond Why not?
Julie He knows.
Hammond (*to Trevor*) Well?

Trevor looks away

Julie You all think I was done over by a burglar, don't you?
Hammond We haven't drawn any conclusions yet.
Julie Mind if I phone my mum?
Richard Of course not.

She crosses to the telephone slowly

> *Hector enters* DR *on his way to the garden and is surprised to find her there*

Hector Julie?
Julie Still got your precious room, Hector? You were boiling, weren't you, when you thought I might take it from you? I've never seen you so upset. (*She dials a number*)
Hector I'm glad to see you home, Julie.
Julie Don't worry. I'm not staying.

> *Hector exits* UR

> I've been doing a lot of thinking back there. Couldn't sleep much the last few nights. Things have gone round and round in my mind. (*She turns back to the telephone*) Mum?... Yeah.... I'm out... I

Act II, Scene 1

want to come home. . . . Yeah. . . . I'm all right, just a bit done in . . . To tell the truth I feel as if I've bin in some disaster movie. I just want to come home for a little while.

Sarah She should never have been released.
Hammond She wasn't released.
Sarah Look at her.
Julie I'll share. . . . I'll share the room. . . . Please. . . . Please, will you talk it over with Dad? . . . I'll ring you later. (*She puts the telephone down and turns* DC)

Richard steps forward to assist her. She shuns him. Sarah moves across to help

Lay off, Richard. I never quite got over the way you helped me once before. Remember? After a couple of brandies and Cokes, we clambered into the back seat of your car.

Sarah What?
Julie "You must try it, Julie. It's the most wonderful feeling in the world."
Sarah Richard?

Richard, confounded and embarrassed, turns away

Julie I thought a lot about that in hospital. Did that trouble you afterwards, I wondered. Did it leave you with any guilt or fear? Because Sarah would be most upset if she knew. Alternatively, I thought maybe Sarah had sussed it out and blamed me. You never know. I kept telling myself I ought to find out about such things.
Sarah What's she saying?!
Richard She doesn't know what she's saying.
Trevor (*moving to the kitchen* UL; *pointing at Julie*) She's paranoid!
Julie When you're in hospital there's not much else to do but read and think, and I never felt much like reading.
Hammond (*moving up*) You ought to go back to the hospital, Julie.
Julie No thanks.
Hammond The doctor wants you to return.
Julie Does he? Will you phone for a mini cab, for me, Sarah? I'm going to stay with my friend Melinda tonight.

Sarah does as she is asked

Hammond Look, I've got a car outside.
Julie Catch me in a copper's car.

Hammond You're being very silly.
Sarah D'you want to go up to your room to rest?
Julie Can't bear that room. The walls are too thin. (*She looks pointedly at Trevor, then turns to the sergeant*) So you don't know who attacked me?

Sarah talks on the telephone quietly in the background

Hammond We're doing our best to find out.
Julie You've done nothing.
Hammond Well then, d'you mind going over a couple of things with me? Seeing as you've dismissed yourself from hospital, and made insinuations; d'you mind?
Julie I've told you everything. What else can I say?
Hammond You never know.
Richard Is this necessary? She's not well.
Hammond We'll take it gently. Sit down.

Julie sits in the armchair C. Trevor will make his way back DL chewing a piece of bread during the following

Now, on the night you were attacked you had previously been in this room. Who was with you?
Julie He was. (*She nods at Trevor*)
Hammond What happened? Did he assault you in any way?
Julie I told you all this.
Sarah (*on the phone*) Oak Avenue . . . sixty-two.
Hammond If you can bear to, I'd like to hear it just once more. Did he assault you in any way?
Julie Not then.
Trevor (*exasperated*) What d'you mean?
Hammond Did he touch you?
Julie Not really . . .
Sarah (*on the phone*) As soon as possible, please.
Julie He tried to make out, though.
Hammond Did you encourage him?
Julie I told him to clear off.
Hammond And did he?
Julie Looked like it at the time.
Sarah Thank you. (*She hangs up*)
Hammond (*demonstrating*) So he went out of the door. You were left alone. Then you made a phone call. Afterwards, you turned out the

lights. There. You were about to go out when you remembered that you hadn't bolted the back door. You went to the back door . . . Right?

Julie nods

But before you got there a man burst in and . . . attacked you.

Pause

Julie (*distressed*) Yes.
Richard I don't think she's up to this, Sergeant.
Hammond She's up to leaving hospital. (*To Julie*) Now then, your assailant. How tall was he . . .? How tall in relation to you? You must have some idea . . . Was he thick set . . .? Muscular . . .?

Julie shrugs

Did you see his hands . . .? Did he wear a ring?
Sarah Sergeant, she's not very well.
Hammond Did he wear a ring, Julie?

Julie looks at her fingers and touches her head

Think, Julie. Think. A ring. Was he wearing a ring?
Julie Yeah. He was. (*She looks at Trevor*) And that's the ring that did the damage.
Trevor (*angrily, moving towards Julie*) You're off your trolley!

Julie hurls herself at Trevor, clawing and flailing. Trevor folds up, making no attempt to hit back. Sarah and Hammond move to pull her away

Get off! Get off!
Julie I can see you now! All your fine talk! To one end, that's all!
Trevor What d'you want?
Julie You never could keep your eyes off me!
Trevor Get lost! You think you're special? You think I'd really put myself out for you!

Hector enters UR

Sergeant Hammond, aided by Sarah, pulls Julie off Trevor. Sarah moves UC

Hector What is it? What the——

Julie You're despicable! I should have really kicked you in the nuts, then you wouldn't want to have a go at anybody else!

Hammond That's enough! Let's get her to her room until the cab arrives.

Julie (*brushing them aside*) Oh, let me leave. Let me get out of this place. I can't bear to be here any longer. I shouldn't have come back! This house, it's, it's awful. I must get away.

Trevor She really is, that one. (*He shakes his head. To Julie*) Got too much sand in her ready mix, that's her problem.

Sarah Trevor!

Dementedly Julie hurls herself on him again

Julie You rotten, filthy . . . I'll claw your——

Trevor Get off! (*This time he is ready for her and hurls her back*)

Julie staggers and limply falls to the floor

Get up! Look at her! Miss Deepfreeze, London North!

The others are staring at Julie, who has not moved

Sarah Julie . . .

WPS Hammond drops to her knees beside Julie and feels her pulse. The others look on somewhat dazed

Hammond She's . . . (*She leans across Julie and listens to her heart*)

Sarah Is she all right?

Hammond works harder to revive her

Richard Sergeant?

Trevor (*quietly*) Send for an ambulance.

Sarah She needs a doctor! (*She moves to the telephone and looks to the sergeant for instructions*)

Hammond (*looking up; quietly*) Get an ambulance.

WPS Hammond bends over Julie again to administer first aid. Sarah hurriedly dials "999"

CURTAIN

Scene 2

Same day, early afternoon

Trevor sits DR. *Richard sits above the table, Sarah below it* L

Richard She must have caught a bus to get here. What goes past the hospital?
Trevor Number six.
Sarah She didn't have any money.
Richard She couldn't have walked.
Trevor I didn't see a cab outside, did you?
Sarah I didn't look.
Trevor When I hit her——
Sarah You pushed her, that's all.
Trevor Well, I had no idea she was . . . so . . . fragile. I had no idea. I mean, she was having a go at all of us, being vindictive and nasty, I thought she had to be feeling good, you know.

Richard rises and turns to the drinks table

Sarah It wasn't your fault, Trevor.
Trevor I knocked her down.
Sarah She attacked you.
Trevor She's back in hospital in a bad way; that's down to me.
Sarah You're not to blame. Whoever beat her up her that night caused the damage. You needn't feel guilty.

Richard moves forward with the bottle of whisky and a couple of glasses

Richard (*to Trevor*) Have a drink. On the house. (*He is about to pour when he is distracted by the low-level content of the bottle. He holds it up to examine it. Without pouring, he continues talking*) We've got to erase all that's happened here.
Sarah Haven't we just. After all, Julie made all sorts of accusations.
Richard She was highly strung. Not accountable. That wasn't the Julie we've known, was it?
Sarah (*dryly*) No.
Richard There was no truth——
Sarah About what?
Richard She was deranged.
Trevor The fact is she's back in hospital.

Richard She'll be all right.
Sarah Let's hope so.
Richard First thing Monday this place is going on the market. Sarah, I've had enough of it. You've just got to put the dust cover over your memories.
Sarah Easy as that, eh?
Richard I know what's worrying you——
Sarah Julie's worrying me——
Richard (*moving closer to Sarah*) —I know what's really worrying you. Take my word for it, there was nothing between Julie and me.
Trevor And if there had been, what's one night's indiscretion, in the back of a car? (*He rises, relieves Richard of the whisky and pours himself a drink*)
Sarah Adultery.
Richard You think your father was so marvellous. (*He points to the portrait*) Playmate for the children. Terrific raconteur. But devoted to the fillies—four legs and two!
Sarah What are you getting at?
Richard I'm just saying . . . your father was absolved. He could put half a nunnery in the club during vespers, and it'd be seen as a careless, sporting gesture. (*He moves away from the picture and turns* UL)

The front doorbell rings

   Sarah exits DL *to answer it*

Richard now takes back the whisky and pours himself a drink. Trevor resumes his seat DR*. Richard turns* UC*. He looks back at Trevor. They exchange a look of incipient sympathy but can find nothing to say to each other. Richard spreads his arms in a hopeless gesture. Trevor raises his glass*

Trevor (*dryly*) Cheers.

Richard nods. They drink

Richard So you feel guilty?
Trevor Yes.
Richard What sort of feeling's that?
Trevor I know I'm alive.

   WPS Hammond enters DL *followed by Sarah*

Act II, Scene 2

Sarah How is she?

Hammond She's still in intensive care: stable but serious.

WPS Hammond looks thoughtfully at the back door, then crosses to the spot where Julie fell. Richard sits UL

One thing's been puzzling me. It appears that as Julie went to lock the back door somebody burst in. It's doubtful if a burglar would break in, assault the occupant and then leave empty-handed, don't you think?

Richard Unless he was disturbed.

Hammond By whom?

Richard She was an attractive girl.

Sarah But she wasn't sexually assaulted?

Hammond No.

Sarah What are you implying, Sergeant?

Hammond It's only a theory. (*She returns to* C) You see, Julie thought that he (*she nods towards Trevor*) attacked her. They had a tiff just after you left. He tried it on. Got rebuffed. Julie said he was wound up. She thought he went round the back to watch her . . . But I have to admit we have no real evidence to support that . . .

Trevor I've admitted I fancied her. And I've told you what happened.

Hammond So did she.

Sarah Why should Trevor want to attack her?

Hammond (*to Trevor*) Why would you? Let's see. You'd been rejected. Your pride had been hurt.

Trevor What pride? I own what I stand up in. Social security just about keeps a roof over my head. I've no job. No prospects. And I'm one step away from joining the swept-aways under the arches.

Hector enters DR

We both are, aren't we, Hector?

Hector What?

Trevor You heard.

Sarah We're ordinary people here. This isn't exactly "The Lower Depths". We may argue among ourselves but we don't knock each other about.

Hector crosses to the kitchen area

Hammond There is another angle . . . Did it never occur to you that Julie might have been mistaken for someone else. . . . It's not so

improbable. I gather she used to go out most evenings. It was unlikely for her to be in this room at that hour. Whereas . . . (*She turns away* UR) It's just a theory. (*She smiles*) C.I.D. stuff.
Richard Wait a minute. You think the attack was meant for Sarah?
Sarah Sergeant, I can't . . .
Hammond What?

Sarah is lost for words

You can't come to terms with that?
Sarah Why should anyone want to attack me?
Hammond Any more than they would want to attack Julie? The probability just sits better, that's all. Think about it. I'd like to check out the back garden again. D'you mind?

WPS Hammond opens the back door. There is the usual noise from next door's stereo

She exits, closing the door behind her

Richard That's a crazy idea.
Sarah Why should anyone want to attack me?
Richard It's only a supposition.
Sarah And if it's not?
Trevor Don't worry about it, Sarah. It's hardly likely there'll be another attack here. At least, not for some time. Hector could probably give you the statistics, the odds against——
Sarah But if somebody wanted to hurt me . . .
Hector Who'd want to hurt you, Sarah?
Richard The Sergeant's got it wrong, as usual. Now look. Listen to me——
Sarah I don't think I know you anymore. This place has changed. Nothing can be taken for granted, can it? What is the reality? What do we know of each other? Was my father really the man you say? He was always so kind and such fun.
Richard Yes, never meant anybody any harm. Created havoc. Even so——
Sarah And Mum? Did she go along with it all?
Richard She was sensible. She preserved the happy home. That meant more to her than anything. The home.
Sarah Keep mum, eh?
Richard What?

Act II, Scene 2

Sarah Keep mum.
Hector What do you mean, Sarah?
Sarah Forget what Julie said. Forget the past. All our pasts. And don't mention the phone call from next door.

She exits DL, *followed by Richard*

Richard (*as he goes*) Sarah!
Trevor What d'you make of it?
Hector Don't know.
Trevor Why did you keep those newspaper reports? It couldn't be from shame. You know what? I think you enjoyed your brief spell in the limelight. I've been meaning to ask you. Hope you don't mind. How did you come to kill your sister of all people? I'd really like to know. No fooling. Come on, sit down and tell me.

Hector sits L *of the coffee table. He looks up for reassurance*

Confession is good for the soul . . . Keeps priests and gossip columnists in work . . . Makes old women happy. Got a lot going for it. Of course, it's better if you confess to a stranger. And despite everything, we remain strangers.

Pause

Hector My sister was older than I was. She had to bring me up because Mum had died early. She never liked me. Not from birth. Even my name, Hector. Hector! She was allowed to choose it. And she did. Out of spite. When I was a nipper she bullied me . . . Years later when Dad died she reckoned to get me out. But I was going to stay in my house. I'd been in my room thirty-two years. Yes. Why should I move?
Trevor (*crossing to the drinks cabinet*) What did you do?
Hector You read the reports.
Trevor Not properly. Only had a glimpse. Go on, Hector.
Hector It was on a Saturday afternoon. In the middle of summer it was. I sat in the kitchen. Having myself a slice of bread and jam. She came in grinning. "You've got a week's notice," she said. "I'm getting married and I want you out." I picked up the bread knife and stabbed her through her blouse. I stabbed her a few times to make sure she was dead. Then I had a wash, changed my clothes, went to the police station and told them what I'd done.
Trevor Have you ever regretted it? (*He moves* DR)

Hector No.

Trevor Must have been rough, being locked away for so long.

Hector You go brain dead for a while. There's an easy way and a hard way. I found the easy way was to stop thinking. After six or seven years you start the count-down.

Sarah enters UL followed by Richard, who remains DL

Sarah Well, that's how I feel! (*She crosses the room and opens the back door*) Sergeant!

Trevor slips off DR

Richard I hope you know what you're doing, Sarah?

Sarah For once, at last, I do.

Richard Consider the consequences.

WPS Hammond enters UR

Sarah Do you really think Julie was mistaken for me?

Hammond Yes.

Sarah By an opportunist burglar?

Hammond Hardly.

Sarah Then who was it?

Hammond You tell me? Tell me anything at all which could help us with our enquiries. We have to find the truth, however unpleasant.

Richard Who's to profit from the truth? You? Will it help your career to know?

Hammond (*moving DR*) What I find really distressing in this job, Mr Higgs, is that I doubt whether my father and certainly not my grandfather would ever have been asked such a question.

Sarah I had a phone call on the night of the attack. Quite late it was. I was just going to bed. The caller was from next door. He said that he'd seen the attacker in the garden and that it was someone from this house.

Hammond Did he say who?

Sarah No.

Hammond Why haven't you told me this before?

Sarah They may well have been trying to wind me up.

Hammond I should be the judge of that. You should have told me.

Sarah (*nervy*) Don't you adopt that tone with me! I'm the innocent party!

Pause

Act II, Scene 2

Hammond Could you identify the voice?
Sarah There's about six guys live next door. Could have been any one of them.
Hammond Just show me the house, will you? Please.

WPS Hammond and Sarah exit UR

Hector Make you feel guilty, don't they?

Richard takes the bottle of whisky from the trolley

Richard (*holding up bottle*) I'm digging into this today.
Hector No wonder. It's the stress. I feel pretty uneasy myself.
Richard Why? What have you done?
Hector Nothing.
Richard So what's troubling you?
Hector Not a thing.
Richard You look worried.
Hector Well, wouldn't you be?

Richard sits on the chair RC. He hands Hector a whisky

Richard I was convinced an opportunist burglar was the culprit. Now I'm not so sure . . . You'd had a few drinks on the night, hadn't you? I mean, you'd been down to the pub. (*He drinks*) You do remember?
Hector Course I do.
Richard Because I know how you enjoy a tipple. (*He replenishes his glass*) I've known you come back here out of your skin. Not often. But I've known it. Now, when you're sober, you're a gem. But when you're pissed, well, one's personality can change when one's pissed. Were you sober or pissed that night, Hector . . .? Well?
Hector I'd had a couple early on.
Richard Just a couple?
Hector I lied to her . . . (*He crosses DL*) I told her I only had one pint that night. Yes. She'll find out I had more than one, won't she? She'll make enquiries at *The Green Man*. She knows I was there.
Richard How much did you have to drink, Hector?
Hector I was sober.
Richard How much?
Hector Three, maybe. I drank fast. I can't remember.
Richard (*following Hector*) Well, if you can't remember how much you drank it follows that you may not clearly recall what you did

later. I'm only pointing out to you, you understand, the weakness of your case.

Hector I'd remember if I'd done such a thing.

Richard Sure you would.

Hector I'd remember that all right. (*He sits* R *of the table*)

Richard (*sitting at the top of the table*) You really ought not to booze as much as you do. You guzzle every night up there in your room. Happy as a sparrow in a bird bath.

Hector It's my one pleasure in life. Yes. So I resort to a little drinkie to pass the hours. I don't cause a nuisance, and I don't believe a few beers makes me aggressive, like some.

Richard You don't believe?

Hector I was upset that night, so I had a few more than usual.

Richard What had upset you?

Hector It don't matter.

Richard Tell me.

Hector (*pointing off*) Trevor had gone into my room uninvited . . . He'd gone down my things, would you believe it?

Richard That's a disgrace. What things did he go down?

Hector Private things. (*He breaks* DC)

Pause

Richard It does tend to put you in the frame though, doesn't it? Being niggled; angry. When you're really upset you could lash out at anybody. Couldn't you, Hector? (*He moves* C)

Hector I was . . . I was angry, yes, but I wouldn't——

Richard —Kill anyone . . .? Again.

Hector Richard—What do you mean, "again"?

Richard Drink leads to violence. By your own admission you were upset that night. (*He closes in* DC)

Hector You said "again". You said "again".

Richard Yes, I did.

Hector Sarah told you. About me.

Richard You're a psycho, Hector. She is a little worried about that.

Hector I'd never harm Sarah! I help her. (*He breaks* L) I wash up. Empty the rubbish. Do the Hoovering. Pop out for things. (*Agitated, he moves around*)

Richard When you killed your sister. I bet you remember that clearly. Do you recall the knife going in? Was it messy? Did you have to put the knife in several times? Did you touch a bone? (*He leans over*

Act II, Scene 2

Hector) I'm told that when you touch a bone it can be tricky. You have to keep putting the knife in. To puncture the vital organs. Was there much blood? What was her face like as she fell back? I bet her face was a treat. She couldn't believe it, could she? Did she cry out?

Hector tries to escape via the door DR *but again Richard cuts off his retreat*

There must have been a swamp of blood. All over her, over the floor, over yourself. Sticky. Hector, did it take you long to forget the blood, that look, that cry? Eh? Can you erase that?

Hector As long as I'm in . . . As long as I'm in a settled, a stable environment.

Richard But you haven't got that here . . . anymore.

Hector This is my home.

Richard Not anymore.

Hector I'm going to my room.

He attempts to move DL *but Richard detains him*

Richard *Your* room? Sorry to say this, Hector, but I have to give you notice, with immediate effect.

Hector What?

Richard For my wife's sake.

Hector (*shaking his head*) No . . .

Richard 'Fraid so.

Hector I'm . . . going to my . . . Excuse me . . . I must.

He turns away and exits DL

Richard Of course, I'll give you a full month's notice. (*He follows Hector*) To get yourself (*as he exits*) fixed up!

He exits DL. *Sarah enters* DL. *She looks behind her*

Sarah Richard?

She looks back through the door then gently closes it behind her. As the evening draws in, so the room has become darker. She is about to switch on the light but is distracted by a sound in the lodger's kitchen and crosses to look inside. Her movements have unintentionally become a replica of Julie's at the end of Act II, Scene 2. She now moves to the telephone and dials a number.

(*On the phone*) Hallo? . . . David? . . . It's Sarah. . . . I'm fine. . . .

And you? . . . Is Louise there? . . . No, it's nothing urgent. Just felt I wanted a chat. I'll ring her later. . . . I'll do that. About seven. . . . Bye, David. (*She hangs up and stands thoughtfully by the telephone for a moment*)

Meanwhile, a silhouette appears against the window and then ducks down

She is obviously worried about the present imbroglio. For a moment she stands in front of the window looking reflectively at the table. She steps forward, leaving her back to the door, which now opens. An arm is extended and the hand covers her mouth as she starts to scream

The intruder is Trevor. Slowly he takes his hand away from her mouth

Trevor Quiet, Sarah.
Sarah Let me go.
Trevor It's all right.
Sarah Let me go.
Trevor Quiet now. You'll get me locked up.
Sarah (*exasperated*) What were you doing?
Trevor Trying it out—not trying it on.
Sarah What?
Trevor You really do feel evil when you steal up to a window or a door in twilight. I wanted to feel the sensation, reconstruct the moment, as it were. Finding you was a bonus. Holding you in my arms.
Sarah Let me go.
Trevor (*softly*) Must I . . .?
Sarah Please.

He releases her

(*Breaking* DRC) You idiot!
Trevor I shall always treasure our moments together, that night, you know; the night Julie was attacked. I was feeling fraught for a while there. You stayed and comforted me. I shall always remember that. From fraught to rapture via a few kind words.
Sarah I never know how to take you. I never know whether you're joking or serious——
Trevor I'm serious——
Sarah (*a touch wild*) —drunk or sober——
Trevor —sober.
Sarah —sane or mad.
Trevor Ah!

Sarah What do mean, "Ah!"?
Trevor Toss you for it.

Sarah's own tension now cracks before Trevor's quirky reactions

Sarah Trevor! Enough! I . . . have . . . had enough. Of your . . . of you, of you all! Somebody here wanted to attack me! Murder me. One of you. The Sergeant is perhaps at this moment finding out which one. I'm worried sick and you come through that door . . .
Trevor Sorry. But it was worth it.
Sarah Was it? Is that how you get your kicks?
Trevor I like you annoyed. I wouldn't be surprised if I didn't love you.
Sarah Aren't you worried about what the Sergeant might be finding——
Trevor I wouldn't be surprised at all.
Sarah You'd love me for a week, a month perhaps, passionately, devotedly; but then what?
Trevor I could love you forever. Have you any bread to spare?
Sarah Help yourself.
Trevor A little cheese. (*He crosses to the alcove and looks around*)
Sarah Whatever you want.
Trevor Some pickle. I've lost my appetite! (*He turns round abruptly*) I want to forget Julie but I can't. Her collapsing like that. I try to be cool, indifferent. I'm not. (*He breaks off a piece of bread and stuffs it in his mouth*)
Sarah I don't understand. Our awful neighbours! Why are they getting involved? Why should they point the finger?
Trevor For kicks.
Sarah Is that all?
Trevor It's enough.
Sarah It's diabolical. "For kicks"!

Richard enters DL

Richard The Sergeant's on her way back. She's got a copper posted in the alley. There's a squad car out front.
Sarah Let her in then.
Richard The door's on the jar.

Silence. They wait apprehensively for the Sergeant's return

Trevor Tick tock . . . tick tock . . . tick tock. That's three tick tocks of our life gone. Never to be retrieved. Makes a mockery of endeavour, don't it? All the time we're accumulating, we're running out of tick tocks.

WPS Hammond enters UR

Sarah Well?

Hammond (*quietly*) I've spoken to the gentleman next door. He's clear about the identity of the man he saw in the garden on the night and at the time of the assault... His description supports the victim's own accusations... (*She puts her hand on Trevor's shoulder*) Mr Billingham, I'm arresting you for the assault on Julie Pringle. You do not have to say anything unless you wish to do so but what you do say may be given in evidence.

Pause

Sarah Sergeant, you're wrong.
Hammond I don't think so.
Sarah Trevor would never hurt me.
Hammond The attack was made on Miss Pringle.
Sarah It was intended for me!
Trevor Don't worry, Sarah.
Sarah You're not guilty. You know you're not.
Trevor I feel guilty.
Sarah Trevor——
Trevor Should have pulled back. Turned the other cheek.
Hammond There's a squad car outside——
Sarah We know!
Trevor I might as well go today. It's as good or as bad as any other day. Actually, it's quite a nice day, for an arrest.
Sarah Oh Lord——
Trevor It is ordained.
Sarah Nothing is ordained!
Hammond All the evidence points to him.
Trevor Yes. Julie said I was the one. She should know. The guy next door has identified the culprit. And you can bet the police are only too happy to finger the collar of a toe-rag like me.

Trevor holds his hands out to be manacled. WPS Hammond ignores the gesture

My old friend, the suburban Hemingway, once said: "Young

Act II, Scene 2

Trevor, there are those in this world who have to suffer for the rest of us."

Hammond (*to Trevor*) Are you ready?

Trevor I'll be able to polish the inner man a little. You know for a time, I considered becoming a priest, a monk even. I can see myself in a cell.

Sarah Trevor——

Trevor Don't know whether to laugh or cry, do you? (*He nods towards the sergeant*) She fancies me, you know.

Sarah (*turning away*) Trevor, please shut up.

Trevor She wants to handcuff me to the cell bars and then have her sergeant's way with me.

Sarah Trevor . . .! (*She looks helplessly at him*)

Trevor (*to Sarah; softly*) Don't . . . Don't look at me like that. If I thought you cared I'd be really screwed up.

Hammond Have you finished making speeches?

Trevor You want more?

Hammond No, but C.I.D. will . . . at the station.

Trevor moves to Sarah and kisses her

Trevor and WPS Hammond exit DL

Sarah She's wrong.

Richard I don't know.

Sarah He's not guilty.

Richard He's a throwback. In the middle ages he'd have queued to be burnt at the stake . . . It was as if he needed to be accused. (*He opens the back door*) It's quiet.

Sarah Why would he want to attack me?

Richard Maybe Sergeant Hammond read them the rule book on noise abatement. (*He closes the door*)

Sarah He had no reason.

Richard His sort don't need a reason. (*He sits at the table* UL *He takes out his calculator and tots up some figures*)

Sarah Who would want to attack me?

Richard Give it a rest, Sarah.

Sarah Who would have a motive?

Richard It's over.

Pause

Sarah Did you want Julie . . .? Did you enjoy making love to her?

Richard No!
Sarah You didn't . . . enjoy it?

They stare malevolently at each other

Really?
Richard No. That's not——
Sarah Did you want the house?

Hector enters DL

Hector I've just seen them take Trevor away.
Sarah Yes, Hector. He's being charged. Will you make some tea?

Hector goes into the alcove UL *Sarah stares at Richard*

Sarah What are you doing?
Richard Totting up a few details. Takes my mind off things.
Sarah May I see: your calculator. (*She takes the calculator from him and examines it*) There's not a scratch on it. You threw it away when you were angry; yet there's not a mark, not a scratch. (*She returns the calculator to Richard*)
Hector I must say—yes—that morning before the attack I was gardening, and I never found your calculator then.
Richard What is this?
Sarah Hector, you found Julie unconscious. You were here when Trevor got back.
Hector He came in soon after me.
Sarah Did you see him go into the garden?
Hector He went outside. To have a look round. I looked through the window and I saw him pick up something. Yes. That's when he must have found your calculator. Just outside the window.
Sarah And somebody else saw him as well. The guy next door!
Richard Julie identified him.
Sarah Julie was distraught.
Richard I'm your husband, Sarah. Just what are you implying?
Sarah At the time it seemed strange. When Julie attacked Trevor, the Sergeant and I had to pull her off. You just stood there. That's unlike you, Richard. You're never one to hold back. Why didn't you help to restrain her? Were you afraid that if you grabbed Julie it might startle a recollection?
Richard Rubbish!
Sarah No more lies.

Act II, Scene 2

Richard Listen——
Sarah I've lived with too many lies.
Richard If you're thinking that I had an affair with Julie . . .
Sarah One more lie and we're finished.

Pause

Richard (*rising and standing near Sarah*) How can you believe—even imagine—I'm guilty? Just because of a calculator. And because I didn't rush to restrain Julie. What are you thinking of? I know what you're thinking of! It's Trevor, isn't it? I was right all along.
Sarah Yes, it's Trevor. He's the one who's accused.
Richard You were having it off, with that parasite. You want me banged up in a cell so you've got free range here! Cock-a-doodle-doo! No wonder you don't want to sell this house.
Sarah Is that what possessed you on that night? You were jealous? You idiot!
Richard I saw the looks you gave him. The looks. Those meaningful looks . . . When the eyes grow large and you . . . smile. That night, you were down here with him until the early hours.
Sarah We talked; that's all. Trevor badly needs to talk. He needs to . . . confess.
Richard Then let him!
Sarah Why don't you tell me what happened. . . . I know you, Richard. When you bluster it's because you're unsure of yourself. Your salesmen have to take it, but not me. Not anymore.
Richard Sarah. Where are you trying to take us? For God's sake . . . (*He drinks whisky. He puts the glass down*) I've worked desperately hard for this promotion. You know that.
Sarah Yes, I do.
Richard Worked round the clock. I'm now getting the rewards——
Sarah I don't care.
Richard You never did!
Sarah Look at you now, Richard. You're combative, aggressive; that's your nature when you're in a spot, when something . . . irks you. That night, late that night, after the attack you came down and found Trevor and me together. Normally, you'd have blown your top, but you didn't. Why?
Richard You're complaining?
Sarah You were preoccupied, worried, desperate.
Richard I was——

Sarah It's not much in the way of evidence. A calculator, and behaviour patterns which don't add up. To the police you could talk your way out of it, I'm sure; but not to me. I know you.
Richard So why are you trying to . . . to . . . to . . . (*Emotionally wound up, the words stick in his throat*)
Sarah Because another man is charged with your crime.
Richard Trevor!
Sarah It doesn't matter who! One more lie and we're finished.

They stare at each other and he knows that she means it. Richard drinks whisky

Richard It wasn't planned.
Sarah Go on.
Richard Just happened. What am I saying?

He looks round desperately, finally focusing on Sarah who stares at him implacably

I was in a suite overlooking Hyde Park. The M.D. and I celebrated with a bottle of Chivas Regal. He was rather pleased with it. Duty free. I didn't realize how drunk I was until I left him and the cold air hit me . . . I drove home.
Sarah You shouldn't have done.
Richard I drive carefully when I've had a skinfull.
Sarah Even so.
Richard I parked the car round the back and came up the garden, well stoned. Then I saw the silhouettes against the window. You and Trevor embracing. It had to be you, didn't it? You never go out. I turned away. I felt gutted. How dare you! When I was so, so . . . feeling, so great . . . ! I returned to the car. Couldn't believe it. How bloody dare you! I ran back up the garden. The room was dark. Dark. I crashed through the door and lashed out. Blindly . . . It was Julie, wasn't it? When I looked down, it was Julie. I felt her forehead. Tried to find her pulse and couldn't. Couldn't find her pulse. I just couldn't. No pulse. I was sweating . . . Then I heard a key in the door and I panicked. I ran out the back headlong.
Sarah Go on.
Richard Afterwards, I walked the streets like a zombie. Then I slowly came round. I kept repeating like a mantra: "You're a survivor. A survivor. You're a survivor!" I knew I had to return: "business as usual". Hardest job of my life.

Act II, Scene 2

Pause

Sarah What about Trevor?

Richard We'll get him a good lawyer.

Sarah And we live with the lie?

Richard Sarah, we've everything to lose. The lot. Nothing can harm Trevor. He'll enjoy playing the martyr. It's his game.

Sarah Even so . . .

Richard He's found himself.

Sarah In jail.

Richard It's a fulfillment.

Sarah And what do we do about Hector?

Richard Hector . . . (*he turns towards him*)

Hector Lord, you don't have to worry about me. I'm one of the family, aren't I? (*He potters in the kitchen*)

Richard (*turning back to Sarah*) We have to think about ourselves. You talk about Trevor. Trevor. Trevor. Have I been right about you two all along? No, that's absurd——

Sarah I'm thinking of us.

Richard I'll see that he gets a good lawyer. Every possible help. (*He crosses to Hector*) We can trust you, Hector?

Hector Of course. I've told you before I regard myself as family. And this is my home.

Richard Sarah? Sarah, darling. I love you so much I couldn't bear the thought of you being with another man.

Sarah Oh, Richard. (*She shakes her head*)

Richard Family came first with your dad. At the end of the day he saw to it that you were protected and happy, didn't he? And your mother stuck by him because, you know, he never was intentionally bad.

Sarah You promise to get Trevor a good lawyer.

Richard The very best. A good lawyer can turn the law inside out.

Hector begins to hum to himself as he prepares the tea. They turn to look at him. He looks back and smiles

Hector Did you know that Honoré de Balzac, the French writer, claimed that his tea came from the Emperor of China?

Richard I didn't know that, Hector.

Hector It was picked by virgins at sunrise. Yes. I'll be able to keep you amused with these stories, you know. I've got a fund of them. (*He busies himself making tea*)

Sarah What are we going to do?
Richard I said I'd get him a good lawyer.
Sarah No, Richard. It won't do.
Richard You'll never be able to manage here if I'm banged up.
Sarah I'll sell the house. Buy a cheaper one. Get a job. I can manage.
Richard Sarah . . .
Sarah (*kneeling at his side*) We mustn't be numbed by the big disasters, the hideous crimes. A girl was criminally assaulted, badly injured, in our home. Goodness, that matters. And a friend has been wrongfully accused of the attack. That matters. Doesn't it? If we don't accept *that*, we're frauds. If there's to be a change for the better for us, it has to start here . . . with ourselves; whatever the cost.
Richard I don't believe in fine speeches. They're outmoded.
Sarah Well, that's me. I hold to old values. I haven't discovered any new ones.
Richard (*sighing, hopeless now, and looking away*) If I go to prison it will ruin my career. Our prosperity will be dead. You'll end up having to sell the house. And all for what?
Sarah You don't know?
Hector Sarah, if the likes——
Sarah (*quietly*) Shut up, Hector.

Sarah stands behind Richard and puts her arms round his neck. He clings to her like a child

Sarah (*softly; to Richard*) Well . . .?
Richard (*quiet, hopelessly*) I'm a survivor. (*He smiles grimly*)
Sarah Richard?
Richard I'm a survivor.
Sarah You can still be.
Richard Not without you.
Sarah It's our problem.

Pause

Richard I could press on. As if nothing had happened. I haven't got a conscience, Sarah.
Sarah I have.

Pause. He succumbs and nods. She kisses the top of his head then moves to the telephone where she dials a number

Sarah (*on the phone*) Hallo? Police? . . . Is WPS Hammond there, please? My husband has something to tell her. . . . It's Mrs Richard Higgs. (*She turns to look at Richard and extends the receiver towards him*)

The Lights fade, leaving her silhouette focused against the window

CURTAIN

FURNITURE AND PROPERTIES LIST

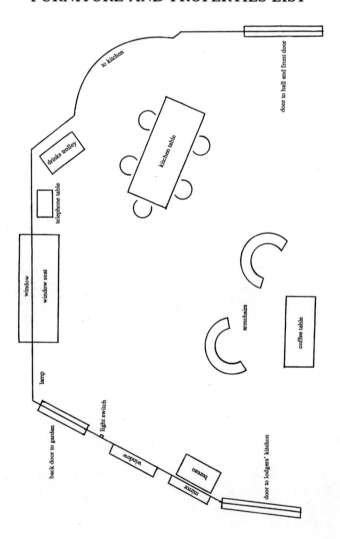

House of Secrets

ACT I

SCENE 1

On stage: Wall mirror
Bureau. *On it*: photograph of **Sarah's** father
Lamp
Window seat
Telephone table with telephone, notepad and pen
Drinks trolley
Kitchen table with chairs
2 armchairs
Pouffe
Coffee table
Pictures, plates on walls
Coffee mugs in kitchen
An heirloom or two
Newspaper for **Trevor**
Coffee machine in kitchen

Off stage: Waste bin (**Hector**)
Briefcase containing notebook (**Richard**)

Personal: **Richard:** silver calculator
Sarah: handbag containing keys

SCENE 2

On stage: as before

Set: Pocket chess set for **Trevor**

Off stage: Carrier bag full of beer cans (**Hector**)

Personal: **Julie:** handbag
Sarah: handbag containing pen, wrist-watch

SCENE 3

Set: Cigarettes on bureau for **Richard**

Off stage: Bread and bread knife (**Trevor**)

ACT II

SCENE 1

Off stage: Small package containing bath oils (**Hector**)
Mug of coffee (**Sarah**)
Piece of bread (**Trevor**)

Personal: **Julie:** shoulder bag

Scene 2

Off stage: Bread (**Trevor**)

Personal: **Richard:** silver calculator

LIGHTING PLOT

Interior. The same setting throughout

Practical fixtures required: standard lamp
Property fixtures required: nil

ACT I, SCENE 1

To open: Backlight on **Julie**	(Page 1)
Cue 1 **Julie** laughs *Bring up autumn morning effect*	(Page 1)

ACT I, SCENE 2

To open: Bring up early evening effect; turn on standard lamp	(Page 10)
Cue 2 **Julie** turns off the main light *Darken room*	(Page 20)
Cue 3 **Julie** turns off the kitchen light *Darken kitchen area*	(Page 21)
Cue 4 **Julie** crosses to the back door *Faint light through the window*	(Page 21)

ACT I, SCENE 3

To open: Bring up evening effect; turn on standard lamp	(Page 21)

No cues

ACT II, SCENE 1

To open: Bring up morning effect	(Page 36)

No cues

ACT II, SCENE 2

To open: Bring up early afternoon effect; darken very gradually
throughout the scene (Page 49)

Cue 5 **Sarah** hangs up and stands thoughtfully (Page 58)
Backlight on window

Cue 6 **Sarah** extends the receiver towards **Richard** (Page 67)
Fade, leaving backlight on **Sarah**

EFFECTS PLOT

ACT I

Cue 1	**Hector** opens the back door *Pop music from next door; cut when the door is shut*	(Page 1)
Cue 2	**Hector** enters UR *Repeat Cue 1*	(Page 2)
Cue 3	**Trevor** opens the back door *Repeat Cue 1*	(Page 10)
Cue 4	**Trevor:** ". . . I do believe we're out of butter." *Punk music during the scene change*	(Page 10)
Cue 5	**Trevor** exits suddenly *The front door bangs*	(Page 20)
Cue 6	**Julie** screams *Resurgence of pop music*	(Page 21)
Cue 7	**Richard:** "It's absurd." *Doorbell*	(Page 24)
Cue 8	**Trevor:** "Oh yes." *The telephone rings*	(Page 34)
Cue 9	**Trevor** opens the back door *Quiet throb of hard rock music*	(Page 35)

ACT II

Cue 10	**Richard** exits *Repeat Cue 1*	(Page 39)
Cue 11	**Richard:** ". . . for chrissake." *Doorbell*	(Page 42)
Cue 12	**Hammond** opens the back door *Repeat Cue 1*	(Page 43)
Cue 13	**Sarah** brings the coffee across *Front door bangs*	(Page 43)

Cue 14 **Richard:** ". . . careless, sporting gesture." (Page 50)
   Doorbell

Cue 15 **Hammond** opens the back door (Page 52)
   Repeat Cue 1

A licence from PHONOGRAPHIC PERFORMANCES LTD, Ganton House, Ganton Street, London W1, is needed whenever commercial recordings are used.

PRINTED IN GREAT BRITAIN BY
THE LONGDUNN PRESS LTD., BRISTOL.